GW00503679

CONTENTS

	Page
Introduction, by Arthur G. Credland	7
Hull & Grimsby Stern Trawlers, arranged by Company in alphabetical order	30
Index of Registration numbers	124
Building of the Hull fleet, 1961 onwards	125
Building of the Grimsby fleet, 1964 onwards	127
The Decline of the Hull & Grimsby fleets, 1976 onwards	128
Top Freezers and Winners of the Dolphin Bowl	131
Name Index of trawlers	136

The "Arctic Buccaneer" mackerel fishing off Cornwall.
Photo by courtesy of Alec Gill.

THE HULL & GRIMSBY STERN TRAWLING FLEET

1961 — 1988

Compiled by

MICHAEL THOMPSON

With an Introduction by

Arthur G. Credland

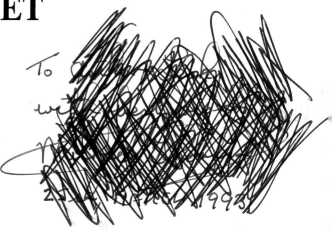

HUTTON PRESS
1988

Published by the Hutton Press Ltd.
130 Canada Drive, Cherry Burton, Beverley
North Humberside HU17 7SB

Printed and Bound by

Clifford Ward & Co. (Bridlington) Ltd.
55 West Street, Bridlington, East Yorkshire
YO15 3DZ

ISBN 0 907033 73 3

This book is dedicated to the memory of the men who lost their lives whilst serving on trawlers, some of whom are remembered in the book; also to the Royal National Mission to Deep-Sea Fishermen, who brought comfort to the families of these men.

ACKNOWLEDGEMENTS

I would like to thank the dozens of people from the fishing communities of Hull and Grimsby for information and support; also Arthur Credland, Keeper of Maritime History, Hull Town Docks Museum; Karon Keating and Jayne Karlsen of Hull Museums for typing the manuscript; the staff of Hull Local History Library and the Technical Library, for their patience whilst finding hundreds of reference items; the staff of Lloyds Register of Shipping; Mrs Conway of H.M. Customs Register of Shipping Department; Malcolm Fussey of Walter Fussey & Son, for providing the basis of the photographs; Adrian Thompson for the artwork.

Lastly the following group of people deserve particular mention for their help with the project: Les Abbey, Peter Abbey, Ian Andrews, Arthur Ball, Gary Bennett, Arthur Blakeston, Bill Brettell, Ray Brooks, John Dobson, Trevor Doyle, Charles Drever, Jonathan Watson Hall, Arthur Hogan, A. (Jacko) Jackson, Jack Noble Kerr, Jack Lilley, Neil Parkes, John Purdy, Harry Smith, Dick Taylor and Terry Thresh.

Sources referred to:
Fishing News, Grimsby Evening Telegraph, Hull Daily Mail, Lloyds Register of Shipping, Olsen's Fisherman's Almanac, Trawling Times.

Mike Thompson
Hull
October 1988

INTRODUCTION

The technique of towing a trawl net over the *side* appeared in the Middle Ages and the same basic principle remained dominant in the European deep sea fishing fleets until the last two decades. Now the 'sidewinder' has been replaced by the stern fishing vessel, often with freezing facilities, for supplying the bulk fish market. The net is towed directly aft of the vessel using a gantry to guide the warps and the full net is winched up a stern ramp from where the catch is emptied down a chute into the fish hold for processing. This approach to fishing was directly inspired by the whale factory ships in which the carcases of the dead whales were hauled up a stern ramp for processing on deck. Introduced by the Norwegian Captain Sörlle in 1925 aboard the *Lancing*, the idea was followed up by the other whaling nations, Salvesens of Leith being the chief British protagonists of modern sub-antarctic whaling.

The expertise gained from their whaling activities resulted in the *Fairtry 1* the first stern-fishing vessel with ramp. Built in 1953 she was too big to berth at any of the nation's fish quays so she usually unloaded her cargo of frozen fillets and meal at the commercial docks in Immingham. After her maiden voyage of 82 days duration in command of Leo Romym, a Bridlington-born skipper, she was redirected, however, to Hull's Alexandra Dock where she arrived in September 1955. She measured 280 feet long with diesel-electric engines developing 2000 b.h.p. and endurance and victualling for three months. The freezing equipment could handle 35 tonnes of cod fillets in 24 hours.

Although technically very successful she was not very profitable and was followed by the slightly smaller *Fairtry 2* (1959) and *Fairtry 3* (1960). From 1960 all quick frozen fish produced by the Salvesen vessels landed at Grimsby or Immingham and 7000-8000 tonnes were handled each year exclusively by Ross Group of Grimsby. In 1966 the price for fish frozen at sea slumped and because of continuing losses these pioneering vessels were withdrawn from service. Salvesens involvement in factory fishing had not been an enormous success and the company decided to concentrate its activities in the areas of cold storage, quick-freezing and transport. They had, however, set a new pattern for fishing which was soon to be followed by trawler firms around the world. Remarkably an attempt at freezing on board ship was made as early as 1884 on the *St. Clement* of Aberdeen. This was built with a cold air refrigeration plant in her aft hold made by J. and E. Hall of Dartford, Kent. It proved very successful and her first voyage grossed a very healthy (for the period!) £117. The system was run off the vessel's main boiler and was removed after a few years operation, though the reasons why are not clear since it seems to have paid for itself and been generally reliable.

It was Halls of Dartford who were to provide the basis for the first significant trials of a shipboard freezing apparatus this century, when the Torry Vertical Plate Freezer was installed in the *Northern Wave* in the summer of 1955. This Grimsby trawler chartered by the White Fish Authority was fitted out in St. Andrew's Dock at Hull, so the two rival ports played their part in this pioneer effort. Costs, estimated at £105,000, were shared between the WFA, the Treasury and the Distant Water Fishing Vessel Owners' Development Committee. The rationale behind these experiments was to avoid the situation whereby huge quantities of fresh fish might be landed simultaneously. The excess of supply over demand depressed prices and resulted in a lot of otherwise edible fish being sent for processing into fish meal. If at least the early part of the catch could be frozen this could be put into storage and released onto the market as required, and when the price was favourable.

In the old side-fishing techniques after the net was brought alongside and the cod end spilled on the deck the net had to be largely man-handled over the side, a dangerous and strenuous exercise. This was eliminated in the stern trawler and for the first time the fish was sorted and gutted under cover protected from the extremes of weather in the North Atlantic. The arrival of the 'stern-dragger', therefore, not only brought a major improvement in technique but provided far better working conditions for the crew.

Freezing also altered the work pattern of the men who unloaded the trawlers, known as 'bobbers' in Hull and 'lumpers' in Grimsby. Instead of filling wooden or metal kits with loose fish in crushed ice, the frozen blocks of fish were passed by conveyor to waiting lorries which delivered the catch into cold-storage.

As opposed to huge 'factory' ships like the *Fairtry* vessels the first stern-fishing trawler on the British register to be built to a more conventional scale was the 104ft Aberdeen vessel, *Universal Star* (1959). Equipped with the now familiar stern gantry, it was unusual in that it could be converted at short notice into a tug. At about the same time Marrs of Hull and Fleetwood began experimenting with freezing at sea, initially by installing a pilot freezer plant, consisting of a small compressor providing refrigeration for a vertical plate freezer, stowed under the whaleback of the *Marbella*. She was a *side-fishing* trawler, built in 1955, and commanded by Charles Drever. The experiments in processing continued on a larger scale in another side-winder, the *Junella*, in which some of the fish hold was used to build a small freezing compartment and a low temperature store. Fish caught in the first 2 or 3 days, about 3000 stones, was frozen and the remainder of the hold filled in the old manner with fish laid on shelves between layers of crushed ice and chilled rather than frozen.

In the event it was Associated Fisheries who introduced the first stern trawler to the Hull fleet. She was the 1226 tonnes (gross), 238 foot *Lord Nelson* which was launched at Bremerhaven on the 5th January 1961 by Frau Rickmer. This handsome vessel was furnished with two holds, one for fresh and the other for frozen fish, with air conditioned cabins, bathrooms, showers and mess room for 24 crew. She sailed on the 19th July 1961 under the command of Skipper Walter Lewis returning on the 24th August from a trip to Greenland and Newfoundland.

The four years of tests by Marrs came to fruition in July 1962 with the launch of the *Junella* at the Hall Rusell yard in Aberdeen. She was Hull's, indeed Britain's, first all freezer trawler with the ability to handle 25 tonnes of fish a day in her newly designed vertical plate freezers. Diesel-electric motors by English Electric powered the vessel and all the processing plant of this 240 foot, 1435 ton vessel. There was the additional facility of blast freezing for large fish such as halibut and up to 300 tonnes storage capacity. The old *Junella,* aboard which the trials had been done, was now renamed *Farnella* and continued fishing until 1966. A series of ten stern freezers were ordered for J. Marr and in 1965 the *Marbella* was launched at Goole. At 284 feet she was bigger than *Junella* with accommodation for 34 crew and a four barrel electric trawl winch which could take up to 1500 fathoms of warp.

In 1964 the *Ross Valiant* became the first Grimsby stern freezer to enter service. She was under the command of Jack Kerr who learned a great deal about the new techniques of gear-handling from his German counterparts who already had several years experience with the stern trawler. As we have seen it was a German yard which provided Hull with the *Lord Nelson,* but the British yards were catching up fast and the *Valiant* was launched by Cochranes of Selby.

Over the years a number of trawlers were exchanged between Hull and Grimsby. The biggest transfer in 1963 involved ten Lord Line side-winders and some 200 crew. In 1978, with the fishing industry in crisis, seven freezers came to Hull from Grimsby, a move which affected over 175 crew. Such wholesale changes of port were deeply unpopular with the men who had to operate away from their home base. They lost time travelling to and from their ships, waiting for their pay settlements and were unable to socialise with their old friends in the local pubs and clubs.

Hellyer's first (of four) all freezer, stern trawler, *Othello* was launched on the Clyde at the Yarrow yard in 1966. An all-welded vessel 224 foot long she was the fourth trawler to bear this name. She had accommodation for 51 men and was designed for fishing in both Arctic and tropical waters. Her duration was up to 58 days with space for a maximum

of 500 tonnes of eviscerated fish. The factory deck allowed space for filleting fish and, if required, she could be turned into a full blown factory ship.

Fire seems to have been a constant refrain in the working history of the stern trawler, several Hull and two Grimsby vessels suffering fire damage.

After the tragic loss in 1968 of three Hull trawlers, the *Ross Cleveland, Kingston Peridot* and *St. Romanus,* all in the space of three weeks, the *Orsino* was taken from her fishing duties to act as guardian to the British trawling fleet operating off Iceland. Provided with a crew of 21 the *Orsino* was able to keep in regular radio contact with her flock and had facilities on board for providing medical treatment for injured seamen.

The introduction of the 12 mile limit by Iceland in 1958, replacing the former 4 mile limit, though it did not greatly reduce opportunities for fishing in northern waters, should have served as a warning signal to the fishing industry. Skirmishing with Icelandic gunboats resulted in the first 'Cod War', but the new limit was officially recognised in 1961 and for a limited period in the season vessels were given access to much of the sea within the 6-12 mile area. Many voices were raised in concern about the conservation of fish stocks and even before the introduction of the new methods of fishing and processing the industry had been bedevilled by overproduction. War losses were quickly made up and there was a dramatic recovery in the fleet size with the trawler owners' eagerness to meet the post-war demand for fish, quickly followed by glut and depressed prices. The awesome catching power of the new stern trawlers made them more cost effective than the side trawlers and they provided the wherewithal for a new market for pre-packed frozen fish and fish fingers. Despite concern about the conservation of fish stocks the industry was buoyant, so much so that a number of companies with no previous involvement in fishing made an entry into the trade. The most notable of these was P. and O. which in the guise of the Ranger Fishing Co. of North Shields commissioned a whole series of stern trawlers between 1964 and 1972.

All the familiar names in Hull fishing invested in stern trawlers, Marrs leading the way as we have seen. 1964 saw the launch of *Cape Kennedy* at Selby for Hudson Brothers. She had accommodation for 28 men and a fish store capable of holding 400 tonnes of frozen fish. The rapidly expanding Ross Group had acquired Hudsons of Hull in 1960 and had commissioned the *Ross Valiant* launched at Selby in 1964 followed by the *Ross Illustrious, Ross Vanguard* and *Ross Implacable.* They also built up a fleet of middle water stern trawlers for Grimsby and the *Ross Fortune* (1965) was only Britain's second 'push-button' vessel for this category of fishing.

Thomas Hamling entered the stern-fishing era with the maiden voyage of the *St Finbarr* in 1964. An all-freezer trawler she was tragically lost after fire broke out in the crew accommodation on Christmas Day 1966. During the blaze 12 of her 25 crew died and she was taken in tow by the *Orsino* which hauled her for nearly forty-eight hours until the rope broke and she finally sank off Newfoundland. Other stern freezers followed in the Hamling fleet, the two sister ships *St Jerome* and *St Jason,* the *St Jasper* and the *St Benedict.* The *St Jasper* was the subject of an experiment during 1972 in the automation of the engine room controls.

1966 saw Boston Fisheries bring the *Sir Fred Parkes* into service as their first freezer and factory trawler followed by the *Lady Parkes,* both built in Aberdeen. A new record for the greatest weight of fish caught in one year was established in 1969, when the *Lady Parkes* landed a total of 4169 tonnes. The Company ordered two vessels, *Boston Lincoln* and *Boston York* from the Gdynia shipyard in Poland in 1968, but both suffered a major design fault which made them rise stern high. As a result the ramp was 18 inches clear of the water and the nets tended to catch on the trailing edge and burst. Each had a crew of 28 with a capacity for 360-400 ton of fresh fish. Two years later *Boston Lincoln* was put into the dry dock of Humber St. Andrew's Engineering Co. to be lengthened by 25 feet and made into a freezer.

Boyd Line ordered the *Arctic Freebooter* which was launched at Goole shipyard in 1965, but she returned from her maiden voyage under the command of Richard Sackville Bryant with mechanical problems.

Throughout the 1960's, fishing and processing was brought to a high degree of technical perfection and though disquiet grew over fish stocks, little was done to establish effective conservation measures by the European nations. The Icelandic government, however, whose only significant national resource is the fish which inhabits the surrounding waters, was determined it was going to retain a larger proportion of the rich cod grounds for the benefit of its own people.

In 1972 they unilaterally declared a fifty mile limit and there followed a period of intense dispute known as the second Cod War, but eventually governments throughout Europe all accepted the new limit. There was deep concern in the fishing industry, but the established firms continued to maintain their fleet numbers either by new orders or by acquiring vessels second-hand.

The Ranger Fishing Co., subsidiary of P. and O., however, was wound up in the face of rising costs and the difficulties caused by restricted quotas. In May 1972 they had lost the *Ranger Ajax* when she caught fire and sank after the crew abandoned ship. Beginning in Autumn 1973 the first of the remaining *Ranger* vessels began to arrive in Hull for their new owners, Hellyers Bros. (B.U.T.). The *Ranger Briseis* had been employed during 1972-3 as one of the trawler support vessels off Iceland and was specially equipped for these duties with an operating theatre and dental facilities. All of these craft received tribal names and contemporary press reports remarked on the luxurious accommodation of the *Kelt* including laundry, video TV and fitted carpets. In February 1974 the former *Ranger Castor*, renamed *Gaul*, was lost off Norway with all hands. She sank without trace in heavy weather and is presumed to have been swamped by waves coming up the stern ramp and entering below decks. The same year saw the building of the *Norse* by Scott and Sons of Bowling with accommodation for 23 crew and a fish hold capacity of 30,000 cubic feet.

Newingtons were appointed managers of *Seafridge Osprey*, an 870 tonnes factory ship built at Aalesund, Norway in April 1972 for Seafridge Ltd. She was followed by *Seafridge Skua* the same year and *Seafridge Petrel* in 1973, all of them filleter factory trawlers. Each had two production lines, a pair of horizontal plate freezers dealing with up to 24 tonnes of frozen fillets a day and a storage capacity of 600 tonnes.

Boyds' *Arctic Buccaneer* (280 foot long, 1173 tonnes) came out of the Gdynia shipyard in Poland in 1973 to become Britain's biggest trawler. She cost nearly one million pounds but suffered from a serious engine fault which delayed her maiden voyage for two years. Designed as a 'go anywhere' vessel to fish in the Atlantic and the tropics, she had a fish hold capacity of 40,500 cubic feet. Deep bilge keels reduced rolling and the bulwarks were extra-high to give better shelter against the wind. In addition she was also heavily strengthened against ice impact. Fitted with smoke detectors and sprinklers, she had accommodation for a crew of 24 in two berth cabins.

The widening of the Icelandic fishing limits encouraged the search for new fishing grounds and the *Boston Lincoln* spent six months off the Argentinian coast engaged in experimental fishing, but was plagued throughout the trip by mechanical problems.

Boston Fisheries took delivery of a fine new ship in 1974, the *Princess Anne* (1476 tonnes) launched at Wallsend on the Tyne, and in 1975 she broke the British record for most fish caught in one year. She was designed to operate in Arctic waters off Labrador, Greenland and Norway to compete against the Russian and German vessels in those ice-filled northern regions. She was the only British built vessel constructed to Lloyds Ice Class 1. Her huge pelagic net could take up to 50 tonnes of fish at a time. The large winch was furnished with two main drums capable of holding 1500 fathoms of 3½ inch steel warp and a further two ancillary drums. The associated net drum would take a complete 'Engel Mode 80' pelagic net, its headline height 120 feet and mouth opening 130 feet.

Iceland's declaration of a 50 mile limit was initially rejected by the European fishing nations but whilst the dispute continued the fleets were confined to restricted 'boxes' under Royal Navy protection and the area of sea available to them was thereby greatly reduced. In spite of these limitations and harassment by gunboats fishing was still remarkably good and *profitable*. Early in October 1973 the new limit was officially recognised and for non-Icelandic vessels access within the new zone was strictly limited. Close seasons were established, and the designation of reserved and conservation areas. Feelings still ran high on both sides and in October 1975 the Icelandic authorities showed their determination to preserve for their own use the seas up to a distance of 200 miles from the shore. The result was further hostilities lasting nearly a year in which the British fleet continued to operate within the forbidden zone guarded by the Royal Navy who gave protection against Icelandic gunboats attempting to cut the trawl warps and generally harass foreign trawlers. Stern-freezers had continued to break catch records but to remain economic had to continue fishing all year round, which the extension of limits militated against. In August 1975 the freezer record fell no less than three times in two weeks, the *St Benedict* (777 tonnes), *Princess Anne* (779 tonnes) and *Arctic Galliard* (845 tonnes). Any attempts to decrease access to traditional fishing grounds or introduction of quotas threatened economic disaster for the trawler companies.

The imposition of the 50 mile limit, although it made inroads into areas traditionally open to British vessels, was most significant as a portent of things to come. As we have seen 1973 saw the acquisition of the *Ranger* fleet by B.U.T. and new vessels were still coming off the stocks indicating the determination of the fishing companies to actively pro-

secute their trade. The 200 mile limit, which was fully recognised in 1977, was a devastating blow by itself but was quickly compounded by other nations following suit. After our entry into the Common Market a resumption of bilateral negotiations between Britain and Iceland became impossible and we were barred from the new zone except for the allocation of a meagre percentage of the *en bloc* quotas granted to the EEC. After December 1976 we were similarly excluded from the White Sea, Barents Sea, Faroes and Norwegian coast, Greenland and Newfoundland. The inevitable result was that a fleet of large highly sophisticated trawlers had few places where they could fish without their activities being severely curtailed by strict fish quotas and limited seasonal access. To add to the economic pressures, a rapid escalation of oil prices by the OPEC countries placed an added burden on trawler owners. When the price rises first began to bite, the oil-fired steamers, the vessels of the side-fishing fleet, were worst affected. They used up to 12 tonnes of heavy oil a day, so inevitably they were laid up in increasing numbers and were hauled off to the breakers' yard often years before their natural working life had ended. Eventually the diesel-powered trawlers were affected too, and in June 1978 the British deep-sea fishing fleet was shrinking at the rate of 2 vessels a week. An additional turn of the screw for the Hull fishing companies, which came at the height of the Cod War, was the closure of St Andrew's Dock, which had been the home of the fishing fleet since 1883. The last vessel to exit through the lock pit was the *Arctic Raider* heading for Spitzbergen at 4 a.m. on the morning of 3 November 1975. Trawlers now tie up in Albert Dock which had been the base of the Hull trawler fleet between 1869 and the opening of St Andrew's Dock.

(Above) The "Fairtry" was the world's first trawler built as a factory ship. The Russians adopted the design for their Puskin class.

The factory trawler, "Ranger Apollo". Photo by courtesy of P. & O. Shipping Co. Ltd.

The "Junella" docks in Hull for the first time on the 11th July 1962. Photo by courtesy of Donald Innes Studio.

The fire-damaged, "Seafridge Osprey", safely back home in Hull.

The "Roman" arriving at Hull after her fire disaster.

A sad end to the fine "Conqueror".

Shorter trips and lower catch rates made the stern trawlers uneconomic and most cod is caught in the North Atlantic between 12-30 miles off shore well within the new limits. Many of these vessels resorted to the mackerel fishing off Scotland and Cornwall, waters not really suitable for manoeuvring large stern trawlers designed for deep sea work. They were not popular either with the inshore fishermen whose preserve this had been.

Arctic Buccaneer and *Arctic Galliard* were also converted in the same year for mackerel fishing and the catches sold mainly to overseas buyers. Exports of this fish by Marrs zoomed from less than half a million pounds worth in 1977 to a remarkable eleven and a half million pounds in 1978. Since the mackerel season off Cornwall terminated on a fixed date and all the boats came back at once facilities for repair, overhaul and refitting were severely over-stretched. As a result many vessels were laid up, at a cost of about £3000 a day. *Seafridge Petrel* was sold to Norway for work in the oil industry, the *Osprey* and *Skua* having preceded it in 1975-6, as a result of the cut backs of quotas granted by Norway to Common Market countries.

The Grimsby fleet was also ailing and high dock charges persuaded their owners to transfer the last seven vessels to Hull in 1978, thus ending the port's direct involvement in stern-freezer fishing.

Fresh fish was being landed in Hull by an increasing number of Icelandic trawlers and there was intense competition between Hull, Grimsby and Fleetwood for Icelandic fresh fish. Growing imports of fish coming into Britain at below market price, however, made it uneconomic for Icelandic vessels to land in Hull.

The closure of the Hull Ice Manufacturing Co. factory in 1978 meant that the last few freshers sailing from Hull were expected to obtain their ice by road from Fleetwood, Grimsby or Aberdeen. In April 1977 the Spanish vessel *Avriscada* was the first foreign *freezer* to land in the port.

In June 1978 the *Goth* was taken into custody by a Danish gunboat accused of fishing illegally for *shrimps* off the West Greenland coast. During the autumn three men died when fire broke out aboard the *Roman* off the Russian coast. Like all the deep sea operators B.U.T. was having a hard time and Associated Fisheries had made a million pounds loss on their fishing activities between October and December 1977 alone. As a result they decided to concentrate their business activities on food processing, cold storage, transport and a range of delicatessen products. By May 1980 Newingtons had sold the last of their Hull fleet. By then the Hull side-winder fleet had ceased to exist, and 27 stern trawlers spent most of their time in the dock. In Fleetwood the Hewett Fishing Co., founded in 1764 and the world's oldest fishing firm, went out of business and Findus closed their Hull frozen food factory with the loss of over 200 jobs, though to balance this move the Birdseye concern was expanding. Marrs were involved in a joint venture in the Baltic involving four of their vessels, a number of Polish trawlers, and the *St Jerome* from Hamling's fleet. In the same year Marrs closed their Grimsby operation but acquired *Subsea 1* for conversion to seismic survey work.

Experienced skippers with modern vessels well equipped for making bumper catches were constantly frustrated by regulations and restrictions. Inevitably there was a temptation to poach and bend the rules, and in May 1980 the *Defiance* was fined a swingeing £52,390 after being boarded by Norwegian fisheries' inspectors, for allegedly using illegal nets inside the 200 mile zone. The skipper, Paul Weeldon, was also fined nearly £2000 before he was allowed to leave Hammerfest. There was also the search for new grounds and new species. In 1979 the *St Loman*, a 223 foot purse-seiner was delivered to Hamlings for use in the blue whiting fishery in the North Atlantic off Faroes. Boyds however had already abandoned this enterprise with losses of a quarter of a million pounds. Newingtons bought a purse-seiner from Norway, renamed *Peter Scott*, and Boyd Line tried pair trawling using the *Arctic Corsair* as the slave vessel working in association with the *Arctic Raider* catching cod and coley in the North Sea. *Cordella* was chartered by the White Fish Authority in the Summer of 1979 for two weeks of test fishing for horse mackerel *(scad)* off Ireland. The *Dane* and *Pict* were converted in 1981 from mackerel to sprat fishing in the North Sea whilst the *Kurd, Arab* and *Kelt* all went to Norway for oil rig stand-by work. The same year the B.U.T. head office was transferred from Hull to Grimsby with a loss of 27 shore staff. They had at this time five freezers fishing in the Barents Sea, five laid up for sale and twelve wet fish vessels operating out of Grimsby in home waters. An attempt to establish a fishing operation out of Albany, West Australia in 1977 had proved a failure; B.U.T. had a 50% share in the Southern Ocean Fish Pty. Ltd. in running the *Orsino, Cassio* and *Othello,* but by 1979 the venture had collapsed. In October 1979 *Ross Vanguard* was sold to Nigeria and *Cassio, Othello* and *Orsino* were planned to follow.

The scarcity of landings meant that in March 1978 the workforce of bobbers in Hull was reduced from 138 to 83 and in 1980 after no trawler had landed for a fortnight all the men were laid off. High dock dues were also putting off potential business and when the Hull Fish Vessel Owners' Association collapsed the bobbers offered themselves for work individually until the formation of the Fish Landing Company. At the same time, the Hull Trawler Officers' Guild reached the brink of closure and overall there seemed to be little future left for the Hull fishing industry. The expansion in inshore fishing did nothing for Hull, but helped to keep Grimsby active and there was a real boom in the Scottish ports. Considerable profits were being made from 'Klondyking', with British vessels selling their catches to Russian and other foreign factory ships without ever landing them in a native port.

The outbreak of the Falklands conflict in 1982 gave an unexpected source of employment for a number of under-used Hull trawlers. *Pict* was requisitioned by the government for mine counter-measures work after returning from Norway with 400 tonnes of frozen cod, haddock etc. After a stint in the South Atlantic she was fishing off West Spitzbergen for shrimps in 1983. The *Kurd* was sold in 1982 to a Norwegian owner, who renamed her *Southern Surveyor* and *Kelt* followed her the next year. After refitting by George Prior Engineering of Great Yarmouth she was able to operate as a mother ship for remote operated vehicles and mini-submersibles. A 'pound' was constructed at the centre of the vessel with direct access to the sea and a dynamic positioning system was installed in the form of two side thrusters at the stern and two at the bow.

The adverse effects of the post-1975 fishing restrictions were less for Marrs than most other companies, thanks to vigorous attempts at diversification and increasing expertise in survey work. The *Criscilla* made her first trip in this role in 1976 with a two month stint in the North Sea, and in 1977 she was chartered to BP for eight months. She was permanently refitted as a survey vessel at a cost of £250,000 and in March 1978 was contracted to Sonar Marine to make a geographical survey of the Brent oil field. The following year she was sold for experimental work to the Royal Aeronautical Establishment. The *Cordella* was chartered in 1979 by the White Fish Authority to evaluate the possibility of setting up a horse mackerel fishery off South West Ireland, and *Cordella, Junella* and *Farnella* were requisitioned along with the *Pict* for minesweeping off the Falklands where they found three of Hull's United Towing fleet on active service too, namely the *Salvageman, Yorkshireman* and *Irishman.* 1984 saw *Cordella* sail to New Zealand under contract to Skeggs Foods but she returned to Britain where after participation in the mackerel fishery she was eventually consigned to the scrapyard in 1987.

The second stern trawler, named *Junella*, returned from her maiden voyage in March 1976 after a 60 day trip with 600 tonnes of fish. In 1980 Prince Charles spent two days at sea on board her and later the same year she ran aground off Skye fishing for mackerel. She was pulled off by her sister ship *Northella* in atrocious weather conditions.

Junella was involved in the transport of troops and ammunition from the QE2 and Canberra during the Falklands landings and after minesweeping off Port Stanley brought one of the mines back to England for further investigation. Though defused this lethal device was still filled with explosives and after a 700 mile journey it was delivered to the Royal Navy at Rosyth. After her Falklands duty the *Farnella*, stripped of her refrigeration plant and trawling gear and fitted with side scan sonar, undertook a

lengthy survey of the bed of the Indian Ocean, returning in 1984. There followed a three week survey of the ocean floor from the Mexican to the Canadian border for the National Environmental Council and the US Geological Survey. After a brief return to fishing as a 'fresher' *Farnella* embarked on survey work again in 1986 and was equipped with free-fall grab suitable for picking up mineral nodules from the deep. Jointly for the US Geological Survey and the UK Institute of Oceanographic Sciences she embarked on a mission to map a million square miles of the Pacific basin.

Southella was chartered in 1980 by the Department of Agriculture and Fisheries, Scotland, for fishing protection and surveillance duties for which she was based at Leith. Apart from the engine room crew she was officered and manned by department personnel. *Northella* had been refitted at Rosyth in 1982 for Falklands duty and then in July 1983 she was chartered as a guard vessel in the English Channel while a trench-laying barge and anchor-handling tugs prepared the way for a cable linking the English national grid with France. For this operation the hull was painted a bright orange for maximum visibility.

In 1982 the *G.A. Reay* was purchased by Marrs from the Ministry of Agriculture, Fisheries and Food to investigate the possibility of establishing a fishery in the Falklands. Originally the Boyd Line trawler *Arctic Privateer*, she has been acquired by the government and renamed after the first director of the Torry Research Station with the intention of investigating the handling and processing of blue whiting off the west coast of Scotland. There was accommodation for 23 crew and 6 scientists and facilities for experimental handling, freezing and storage. Meantime the omens on the local fishing front remained bad.

Swanella had been chartered to the Fisheries Ministry in 1973 and in January 1980 she was one of four trawlers employed by the White Fish Authority in the search for new fishing grounds.

The sale of vessels continued with *Arctic Galliard* and *Arctic Buccaneer* going to Fletcher Fishing of Auckland, New Zealand, for less than their insurance value. Both vessels had been top fishers; the *Arctic Galliard* caught a port record of 845 tonnes of fish on her maiden voyage and the *Buccaneer* had held the national record for weight of fish caught in one year at a hefty 6272 tonnes.

In October 1983 Boston Fisheries was taken over by the North British Maritime Group which also included the old established Hull tug company of United Towing. The *Lady Parkes* holder of the annual catch record in 1969 at 4169 tonnes had been sold to the Faroes in 1977 and in an attempt at diversification the *Boston Sealance* (1750 tonnes) was built in 1979 as a refrigerated cargo vessel, capable of carrying all kinds of frozen meat and fish. Her first cargo had been one of pork landed at Lisbon from Rotterdam. Boston Offshore Safety Ltd. was established to convert trawlers into North Sea standby vessels for the oil and gas industry; the fleet included the *Boston Sea Fury, Sea Gazelle, Sea Vixen* and *Sea Knight.*

1983 saw the famous old Hull firm of Thomas Hamling go into receivership, a year short of its centenary. The *St Jerome, St Jasper* and *St Jason* were bought by Seaboard Offshore Ltd. of Great Yarmouth and Tain for stand-by work.

Decommissioning grants of £400 per ton became increasingly attractive and in 1984 the *Dane, Norse, Goth, Roman, Defiance* and *Boston Lincoln* were all disposed of. On the other hand Iceland's successful exploitation of their native fish reserves generated plenty of surplus capital for investing abroad and in 1985 the 105 year old Hull-based Brekkes Foods was taken over by an Icelandic company.

A stabilisation in oil prices and increasing government support helped to generate new optimism in the industry. In 1985 the side-winder, *Arctic Corsair*, returned to the sea after four years lay-off. She was fitted out with the help of the London based Inlak Group as joint owners and sailed under the command of Skipper Bernard Wharam. In June 1986 she broke the wet fish landing record for the fourth time with a catch of White Sea cod and codling worth £153,341. *Arctic Corsair* returned from her last voyage on 22 December 1987 and is now laid up awaiting scrap or possible acquisition as a museum ship after a long and honourable career. Boyd Line acquired the 200 foot Norwegian vessel, *Vesturvon*, in 1986 which they renamed *Arctic Ranger* for use as a factory filleting ship off Labrador.

In 1986 Marr and Son was restructured into two companies, Andrew Marr International Ltd. which concentrates on fish processing, vessel maintenance and cold storage, and J. Marr, dealing with wet fish, survey vessels, oil rig supply vessels and the management of Globe Engineering. In August 1986 the fleet consisted of six trawlers and eight survey vessels with an increasing interest and investment in the Falklands. Initially Marrs had chartered ten Japanese squid-jigging vessels but soon opened an office in Port Stanley creating a new company, Marr Falklands Ltd., for future operations. In April 1988, the factory freezer *Hill Cove* operated by Stanmarr Ltd., a joint venture between Stanley Fisheries and Marr (Falklands) Ltd., was named by Mrs Sally Blake, wife of a Falklands Council member. She left Hull loaded with spare fishing gear and other fabrications from Globe Engineering for refurbishing the Falklands port and storage system which the Island's government had bought from the Ministry of Defence.

Boyd Line have also made a significant investment in the South Atlantic and in 1987 Stanley Witte Boyd re-registered the former *Arctic Freebooter* as the *Lord Shackleton*, to work out of Port Stanley for the Falklands Development Council. This as yet infant fishery is initially concentrating on squid and hake as its main quarry. There are currently negotiations in progress to establish a consortium to operate a new ferry service with mainland South America. The partnership includes Stanmarr and Witte-Boyd Holdings and aims to re-establish links severed in 1982 so as to ensure regular supply from Uruguay and Chile to service the fishing vessels and islands in general, and provide an easy outlet for marketing Falklands fish.

In March 1988 Marr acquired the Dutch freezer trawler *Cornelius Vrolijk* for a reported £5 million pounds and renamed her *Westella*. Capable of freezing 120 tonnes of fish a day and with a cold store capacity of 1400 tonnes she will fish herself, but also act as a 'Klondyker' taking catches from other vessels for processing at sea, a mode currently dominated by Eastern bloc vessels. Another sign of the buoyancy and confidence returning to Hull fishing came with the launch of the *Thornella* by Cochranes of Selby in 1987. In March 1988 after fitting out she loaded 100 tonnes of ice from the new £350,000 plant of Hull Fish Landing and Container Services on Albert Dock in readiness for her fishing trials. She landed 1400 kits of coley from off the Shetlands the week before the launch of her sister ship *Lancella* on 18 April 1988. Investment in Marrs' scientific fleet continued with the purchase of the *Jura*, now renamed *Criscilla*, formerly belonging to the Department of Agriculture and Fisheries, Scotland.

No-one doubts the ability of the fishing industry to design the ships and equipment required to operate in any corner of the globe. The big question mark remains whether a satisfactory world wide control of the exploitation of fish stocks can be established. Close to home there are ominous reports of a pending catastrophic decline in the 'cod basket' off the Lofoten Islands where the worst cod season for twenty years has been reported by local fishermen. Later maturity of young fish and weather changes appear to have forced an alteration in the breeding pattern. This has been compounded by a large rise in the seal populations off Western Norway, though these are now being decimated by a virus, and the failure for the last two years of the arrival of capelin, the main food of cod. Carpet trawling has effectively vaccuumed the heartland of the North Sea and Barents Sea and prevented mature cod from reaching the traditional breeding ground off the Lofotens. Vast quantities of young fish which should have been allowed to grow to maturity have instead finished up as fish meal. The estimated stocks in 1955 in the Barents Sea were 4-5 million tonnes, but by 1982 these were down to 1 million tonnes. The large, technologically advanced and capital intensive factory trawlers which need to fish to capacity all year round in order to stay economic are the main culprits and present the same threat to fish stocks as the whale factory fleets have done to the populations of great whales.

Arthur G. Credland
Hull Town Docks Museum
October 1988

AT WORK
A series of photographs taken aboard the "Ross Valiant" by Skipper Jack N. Kerr

Pancake ice.

In the ice off Newfoundland.

(Left) Halibuts for the hold.

(Below) The crew take a break.

(Left) The crew check the headline floats.

(Top)Shooting the trawl under the direction of the Mate. Photo by courtesy of Alan Blenkin.

(Above) Packing fish in the freezers. Photo by courtesy of Alan Blenkin.

THE "HAMMOND INNES"

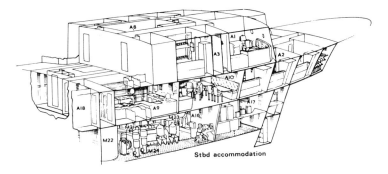

Stbd accommodation

THE VITAL STATISTICS

Length overall : 191 ft.
Breadth moulded : 36 ft. 9 in.
Fishroom Capacity : 19,500 cu. ft.
Complement : Upper deck 7, Lower deck 10
Main engines : Werkspoor 6TM410, 2500 metric bhp at 500 rpm.
Port auxiliary set : 242 kW.
Stbd auxiliary set : 242 kW.
Harbour set : 40 kW with air compressor
Propeller : 4 bladed controllable pitch
     Stones Manganese Marine, 260 max. rpm.
Main winch : Norwinch Hydraulic.
        Type TUD-30-540-140 (split winch).
Net drum : 'Norwinch' Hydraulic
Auxiliary winches : Type MF45 (two).
Windlass : 'Norwinch' Hydraulic Type 1A 27/32.

MISCELLANEOUS
1 Inflatable boat
2 Searchlight
3 Reflector compass
4 Fishing lights
5 Twin radar scanners

SPACES AND ACCESS
A1 Captains accommodation
A2 Crews accommodation
A3 Washrooms, showers, etc.
A4 Wheelhouse
A5 Chart room
A6 Electronics room
A7 Radio room
A8 Recreation room with T.V. and Cinema
A9 Modern mechanised galley
A10 Officers/crews mess
A11 Steering gear compartment
A12 Liver boiler room
A13 Gutting room
A14 Fish room
A15 Shaft tunnel
A16 Engine room
A17 Sound insulated engine control room
A18 Access passage way through fish hold
A19 Chain locker
A20 Ice pounds (port and stbd)

MAIN AND AUXILIARY MACHINERY
Other than deck machinery
M1 Fishroom hatch
M2 Spade rudder
M3 4 bladed controllable pitch propeller
M4 Pitch Control mechanism
M5 Ramp
M6 Ramp doors
M7 Fish hatch
M8 Fish chute
M9 Humber fish washers
M10 Type 28 Shetland gutting machines
M11 Slush well pumps
M12 Deck head cooling grids
M13 Fish room conveyor
M14 Hydraulic pumps for main winch
M15 Gearbox
M16 40 kW harbour duty set
M17 Spanner boiler
M18 Silencer
M19 2500 bhp main engine
M20 242 kW auxiliary set (port)
M21 242 kW auxiliary set (stbd)
M22 Sprinkler air/water bottle
M23 Main engine air receivers
M24 Pumps : fresh water, sea water bilges, lubricating oil, fuel oil, etc.

TANKS AND SOTRES
T1 Net stores
T2 Cod liver oil tank
T3 C.P. drain tank
T4 Oil fuel tanks
T5 Slush wells
T6 Boiler feed water tanks
T7 Cofferdams
T8 Lubricating oil tanks
T9 Fresh water tanks
T10 Water ballast tanks

DECK MACHINERY
D1 Hydraulic anchor windlass
D2 Cable winch for headline transducer
D3 Split hydraulic trawl winch
D4 Trawl warps
D5 Warp tension meters
D6 Hydraulic net drum
D7 Hydraulic auxiliary winches
D8 Stern gantry
D9 Towing blocks (bottom trawls)
D10 Towing blocks (midwater trawls)

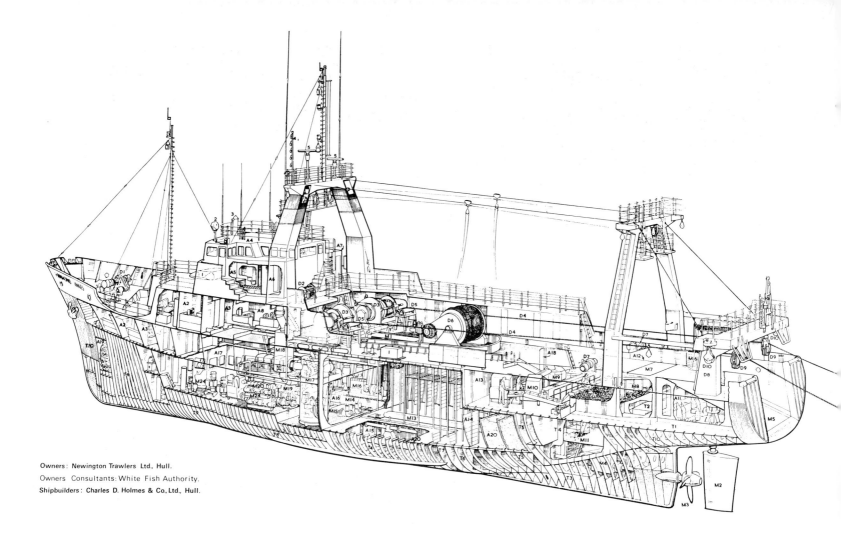

Owners: Newington Trawlers Ltd., Hull.

Owners Consultants: White Fish Authority.

Shipbuilders: Charles D. Holmes & Co., Ltd., Hull.

26

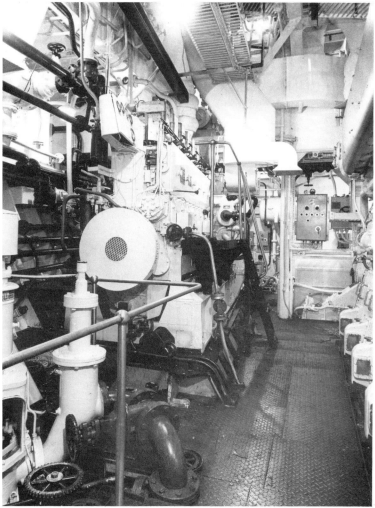

(Above) The bridge of the "Arctic Buccaneer" with
Skipper Michael Landrick (seated) and Mate,
Tony Tuton.

(Right) The engine room of a freezer trawler.

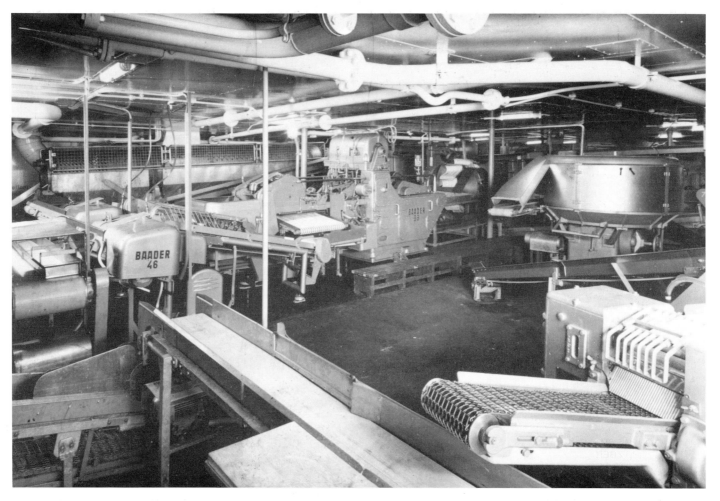

The layout of Baader equipment on a factory freezer. Photo by courtesy of Nordischer Maschinenbau, Lubeck.

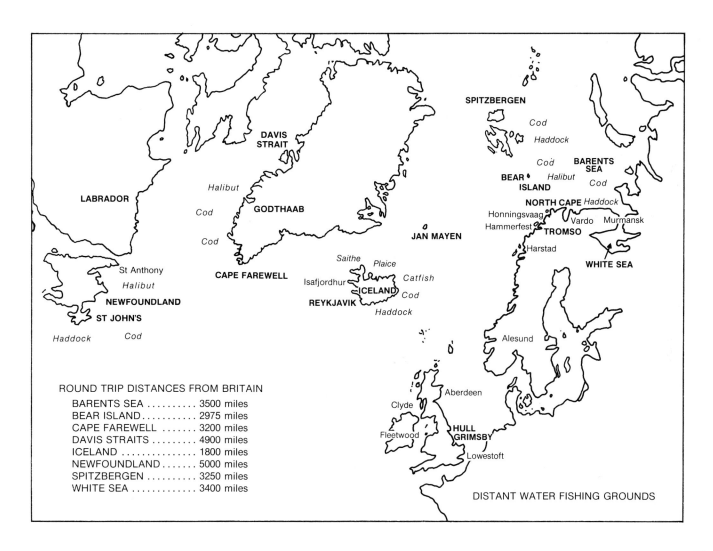

SPITZBERGEN

Cod

Haddock

BARENTS SEA

Cod

DAVIS STRAIT

BEAR ISLAND *Halibut* *Cod*

NORTH CAPE *Haddock*

Halibut

LABRADOR

Cod

GODTHAAB

Cod

Honningsvaag

Hammerfest   Vardo   Murmansk

TROMSO

JAN MAYEN

Harstad

WHITE SEA

St Anthony

Halibut

Saithe

Plaice

CAPE FAREWELL

Catfish

NEWFOUNDLAND

Isafjordhur

ICELAND   *Cod*

ST JOHN'S

REYKJAVIK

Haddock   *Cod*

Haddock

Alesund

ROUND TRIP DISTANCES FROM BRITAIN

BARENTS SEA .... 3500 miles
BEAR ISLAND .... 2975 miles
CAPE FAREWELL .... 3200 miles
DAVIS STRAITS .... 4900 miles
ICELAND .... 1800 miles
NEWFOUNDLAND ...... 5000 miles
SPITZBERGEN .... 3250 miles
WHITE SEA .... 3400 miles

Aberdeen

Clyde

Fleetwood

HULL
GRIMSBY

Lowestoft

DISTANT WATER FISHING GROUNDS

29

ASSOCIATED FISHERIES

Associated Fisheries was registered as a company on the 28th February 1929, by John Bennett, the Billingsgate Fish Merchant whose father had founded the Bennett family fish merchant's business in 1889.

John Bennett Jnr., after leaving school, became the 3rd generation of the family to work at Billingsgate. After serving in the Commando's during the War, he rejoined the firm and in 1949 he took over the management of Northern Trawlers, the Associated Fisheries Grimsby Company and in 1959 became Managing Director of Associated Fisheries.

In 1950 Associated Fisheries acquired Lord Line, the large Hull trawler company, and appointed Thomas W. Boyd as manager.

During 1961 Sir Hugh Fraser took over as Chairman from the retiring Mr. Stewart Cole at the same time as the arrival of the Company's large stern trawler, the "Lord Nelson", and a large expansion programme was planned.

Then in 1963 Associated Fisheries amalgamated with the Hull trawler firm Hellyer Brothers, who took over the running of the Lord Line Fleet.

By 1964 Associated Fisheries had become the largest independent trawler owners in Europe and had ordered 7 more freezer steam trawlers. On the 1st July 1969 they merged with the Ross Group to form British United Trawlers.

LORD LINE
Hull

NAME THEME-:Ships were named after Lords.
FUNNEL:- Black top with white band
HULL:- Green with white line later Hellyers colours

NORTHERN TRAWLERS
Grimsby

Ships had Northern Prefix except freezers which were named after Nelson's ships which fought at Trafalgar.
FUNNEL:- Black top grey with with band
HULL:- Black with white line
Later:- Black top white with a dark blue band below a pale blue band within the blue bands a white 'A' outlined in black

CONQUEROR

Sailed from Grimsby on her maiden voyage on the 30th of December 1965.

In August 1971, after the British fishing fleet had been experiencing lean times Conqueror after a 43 day trip landed 540 tons of fish including 160 tons of plaice. This was the best catch of the year.

Transferred from Grimsby to Hull 19th October 1977.

Name	Reg. No.	Off. No.	Tons	Length/ Breadth	Call Sign
Conqueror	GY 1364	307550	1644	232.6	GRZA
			657	41.1	

Builder	Type
Hall Russell & Co. Ltd. Aberdeen 1965	Wholefish Freezer

Factory Details

27,000 Cu.Ft. Fish Hold
10 L. Sterne V.P. Freezers able to freeze 35 tons per day in 100lb. blocks
Shetland type 28 Gutter (1971).

Engine Details

Mirrlees National Ltd.
Type KLSSMR 8

Launched	Skipper Maiden Voyage	Crew No.
8th September 1965	Colin Newton	29

Named by

Mrs. P. J. Duffen, daughter of Associated Fisheries' Director Mr. J. Llewellyn

The Loss of the Conqueror

Conqueror left Hull to fish off Cornwall on the 13th December 1977, after a refit to add extra freezer space for mackerel fishing. On the 27th December in bad weather at 6-10 am she ran hard aground on rocks at Penjer Point, near Mousehole, Cornwall. The Penlee lifeboat took off her crew except for the skipper and mates who prepared for an attempt to re-float her. Among the ships that stood by to give assistance were the Trinity House vessel "Stella", "Farnella" and the "Junella" which tried to tow her free, but failed.

The salvage tug Biscay Sky arrived on the scene and put heavy pumps on board ready to pump out the water after patches had been placed over holes in Conqueror's hull. The main problem, for the salvors was that a winter gale could blow up and the Conqueror would be pounded on the rocks, so it was a race against time. In an early attempt to pull her free, an escape hatch blew out and water flooded back in again.

Unfortunately when the salvage team was only two days from pulling her free, a sudden gale blew up and left Conqueror with a 45 degree list and submerged from the stern to midships.

On 23rd January 1978 after divers reported she was very

Photo by courtesy of Steve Pulfrey

badly holed, the salvage team packed up their equipment and the Conqueror was abandoned to the sea.

DEFIANCE

Name	Reg. No.	Off. No.	Tons	Length/Breadth	Call Sign
Defiance	GY 1377	307564	1609	232.6	GKSE
			690	41.1	

Builder	Type
J. Lewis & Sons Ltd. Aberdeen 1966	Wholefish freezer

Factory Details

27,000 Cu.Ft. fishhold
10 L. Sterne V.P. freezers able to freeze 35 tons per day in 100lb. blocks.
Halibut Room.

Engine Details

Mirrlees National Ltd.
Type KLSSMR &
2350 BHP   14½ Knots.   .

Launched	Skipper Maiden Voyage	Crew No.
25th June 1966	Bill Ferrand	29

Named by

Mrs. D.V. Biggs, wife of a director of Associated Fisheries.

The Defiance was delivered on November 22nd, but due to engine problems after 3 trials in 2 months she had to go to Immingham for an overhaul.

Defiance sailed on her maiden voyage on the 19th January 1966. Skipper Ferrand took her to the Canadian grounds and after 7 weeks landed 500 tonnes at Grimsby. The Defiance was one of Grimsby's top freezers, well placed in the Dolphin Bowl competition on three occasions.

Defiance became part of the B.U.T. fleet in 1969. On the 30th December 1977 she was transferred from Grimsby to Hull, but retained her Grimsby reg. no.. When she was sold for standby work on the 22nd April 1985, Defiance was the last of the 7 Associated Fisheries freezers to go. Her 2 sisters were lost, the 4 Hellyer ships sold and the Lord Nelson scrapped. She is now laid up in Albert Dock, Hull.

Now Seaquest Defiant
X Defiance 1985.

LORD NELSON

Name	Reg. No.	Off. No.	Tons	Length/ Breadth	Call Sign
Lord Nelson	H 330	301659	1226	221.7	GHCH
			527	36.5	

Builder	Type
Rickmers Werft	Part Fresher
Bremerhaven 1961	Part Freezer

Factory Details

Wetfish Room 12,000 cu.ft.
Frozen fishroom 12,000 cu.ft. able to freeze 25 tons per day in 94lb blocks
2 Banks of Torry Hall V.P. Freezers 16 x 6 station

Engine Details

Mirlees Bickerton & Day
ALSDM6 Turbo 6 Cyl
2000 BHP 16 Knots

Launched	Skipper Maiden Voyage	Crew No.
14th January 1961	Walter Lewis	24

Named by

Frau Rickmer

Lord Nelson was built as an experimental stern trawler. She had 2 fishrooms, the idea being to fill the frozen fish room first and then the normal fresh catch chilled with crushed ice.

Lord Nelson was Hull's first stern trawler. She arrived at Hull on the 30th June 1961 from the German shipbuilder's yard. Lord Nelson was put on display in St Andrew's dock with Lord Line's oldest ship Lord Stanhope which was built in 1935.

Lord Nelson was registered as owned by West Dock S.F. Co. which was an Associated Fisheries' subsidiary company. She passed to Hellyer management in 1963.

Lord Nelson sailed on her maiden voyage on the 19th July 1961. Skipper Lewis took her fishing at Spitzbergen, Barents Sea and Bear Island. After a 36 day trip she landed 48,000 stones, 20,000 fresh, 28,000 frozen in 4,300 blocks.

Whilst outward bound off Cape Wrath in 1963, the crew of the Lord Nelson suffered a stunning tragedy. When her popular mate, Jack Philips, fell off the catwalk into a bitterly cold sea, the cook, Charlie Vine, dived overboard in a bid to help him, but the mate was lost. After being picked up Charlie Vine had to be rushed to hospital at Aberdeen suffering from severe exposure and was lucky to pull through. He was later awarded the Humane Society Medal.

In May 1971 whilst fishing off West Greenland at Fylla Bank commanded by Skipper Norman Longthorpe she was holed by ice. She had a gash several feet long in her port side. Her pumps were able to cope with the intake of water and she steamed 900 miles to Reykjavik in Iceland for repairs.

After she had been laid up in 1980, B.U.T. sold her for scrap. On 15.10.1981 she sailed from Hull fish dock to be scrapped at Draper's scrapyard at Victoria Dock Hull.

Some Details of her Trips

Aug. 1964. Skipper N. Longthorpe 42 days Newfoundland (211³/₄ tons frozen) 2275 kits fresh £6,278.

Aug. 1971. Skipper N. Longthorpe 40 days White Sea (200 tons frozen) 1883 kits £15,261.

Fresher Trips Only

26 June 1973. Skipper N. Longthorpe 22 days White Sea (2563 kits £33,091).

10 April 1975. Skipper N. Longthorpe 19 days White Sea (2728 kits £43.974).

26 Aug. 1975. Skipper P. Atkinson 20 days White Sea (2416 kits £42,709).

10 Dec. 1976. Skipper N. Longthorpe 26 days White Sea (2083 kits £66,105).

17 June 1977. Skipper N. Longthorpe 20 days Bear Island (2037 kits £60,000).

22 May 1978. Skipper J. Russell 24 days Norwegian coast (1998 kits £59,075).

VICTORY

Name	Reg. No.	Off. No.	Tons	Length/ Breadth	Call Sign
Victory	GY 733	304796	1750 664	244.9 41.2	GPPA

Builder	Type
John Lewis & Sons Ltd. Aberdeen 1965	Wholefish Freezer

Factory Details

27,000 Cu.ft.
10 L. Stern U P Freezers able to freeze 35 tons of fish per day in 100lb. blocks

Engine Details

English Electric — Diesel Electric
Type 8 CSRKM
3240 BHP   13¹/₂ Knots.

Launched	Skipper Maiden Voyage	Crew No.
22nd October 1964	Bernard Newton	25

Named by

Lady Fraser, wife of Sir Hugh Fraser, Chairman of Associated Fisheries Ltd.

To complement their Hull based 'Lord Nelson', Associated Fisheries decided to use the names of Admiral Nelson's warships which fought at the Battle of Trafalgar for their Grimsby freezer fleet. To use the warship names Associated applied to the Admiralty for permission, which was granted.

Like the Lord Nelson, the 'Victory' was built for the Associated Fisheries subsidiary company, West Dock Steam Fishing Company of Hull. Victory was given to Northern Trawlers management.

She sailed from Grimsby on her maiden voyage on the 23rd April 1965 and Skipper Newton took her fishing at Greenland, Newfoundland and Labrador. She returned with a record catch of 540 tonnes mainly of cod, in 12,394 100lb. blocks, 11,074 cod, 464 reds, 346 haddock, 252 cats and 258 headless cod. She was away 50 days.

On her 4th voyage she topped this with 547 tonnes, of which 31 tonnes were headless. In autumn 1966 when fishing was slack she fished at White Sea, Bear Island, Greenland and Newfoundland. Although she was away 70 days Skipper Tommy Spall brought back a very respectable 500 tonnes.

In June 1968 Skipper Tommy Spall with mate D. Scott brought Victory home from a fast 31 day trip to the Norwegian coast and White Sea to land 533 tonnes.

The Loss of the Victory

On the 1st May 1974 whilst fishing off Norway, the Victory, commanded by Skipper Wally Wilson, caught fire in the engine room. The engineers were forced to evacuate the engine room and the blaze was put out by the use of CO_2. As the ship was drifting without power, the Hull trawler Kurd with skipper John Dobson came to the Victory and put a line aboard and stood by her through the night. At 0630 Kurd started to tow Victory towards Vardo, Norway. But in the afternoon a 2nd fire broke out, which the Victory's crew were unable to control. So Kurd slipped the tow and took Victory's crew aboard. Meanwhile a Russian warship put a line on Victory, took her in tow and beached her on the west side of the Kola inlet near the port of Murmansk. A few months later insurance surveyors from Grimsby visited the Victory. She had been gutted by the fires and had rolled onto her starboard side and was two thirds submerged. Victory was written off as a loss.

BOSTON DEEP SEA FISHERIES

Boston Deep Sea Fisheries was founded in 1885 by Fred Parkes, who was later knighted for his services to the fishing industry. The Company began operating out of Boston Lincs, with a North Sea trawler fleet.

In 1918 the Company moved to Hull and Fleetwood, then in 1939 the old established St. Andrew's Steam Fishing Co. Ltd. of Hull was acquired and kept alive as a subsidiary company.

After the 1939-1945 War the Company's re-building program began with several new trawlers for the Hull Fleet. Eventually Boston D.S.F. went on to become one of Britain's major fishing companies, thanks to the hard work of Sir Fred Parkes and his son Basil, with interests also in Grimsby, Lowestoft, Milford Haven, France and Canada. In 1966 the Company took delivery of 2 freezer stern trawlers, the first in a fleet of 5.

During 1971 in recognition of his contribution to the fishing industry, Basil Parkes the Company's Chairman received a Knighthood, his title becoming Sir Basil Parkes O.B.E. J.P.

With the demise of the fishing industry the Boston D.S.F. fleet was gradually disposed of, the last trawler going in 1986.

NAME THEME: Boston Prefix, Royalty and Prominent people.
FUNNEL: Black top, cherry red.
HULL: Black.
BOW CREST: Shield containing company crest of 3 crowns.

BOSTON LINCOLN

Name	Reg. No.	Off. No.	Tons	Length/ Breadth	Call Sign
Boston Lincoln *1968*	GY 1399	333948	846 285	212.0 39.4	GYBE
Boston Lincoln *1970*			994 374	237.7 39.4	

Builder	Type
Stocznia Im Komuny Paraskiej Gdynia 1968	Fresher converted to Freezer

Factory Details

21,200 cu.ft. (Fresher)
30,000 cu.ft. (Freezer)
12 Jackstone Froster V.P. Freezers capable of freezing 45 tons per day
Sept 1972 : 2 Baader 433 Headers

Engine Details

Mirrlees National Ltd
Type KLSSMR 8
2600 BHP   15½ knots

Launched	Skipper Maiden Voyage	Crew No.
30th September 1967	W.G. Balls	23-27

Named by
Mrs. E. Tee, wife of Lloyds representative in Poland

Boston Lincoln arrived at her home port of Grimsby on Easter Saturday 1968, from the Polish builders yard. For her maiden voyage Skipper G. Balls took her fishing at Iceland. During the trip considerable difficulty with the trim cut down fishing time to around 5 days. On her return she landed 1713 kits for £8,448.

In 1969 Boston D.S.F. decided to convert Boston Lincoln into a Freezer and lengthen her. In her 9 months as a Fresher she had completed 14 trips and landed 37,163 kits for £152,373. During October 1969 she came into the William Wright Dry Dock at Hull, she was cut in two and a 25′ 7″ section was added midships. This complicated task was completed by Humber St. Andrews Eng. Co. then refrigeration and cold store plant was installed. The total cost was £150,000 and the work was finished in March 1970. Boston Lincoln's first trip as a Freezer began on the 25th April 1970. In July 1971 she transferred to Hull from Grimsby to join Boston D.S.F's other 3 Freezers, to allow the freezer operation to be run from the one port.

Boston Lincoln was chartered in September 1972 by I.F.O.S. Ltd., trawler agents, for a 6 month exploratory trip to the Patagonia fishing grounds off Argentina. She also fished around the Falkland Islands and the voyage was an important exploration which has subsequently led to the present day intensive fishing in the Falkland zone. Her hull was painted white for the tropics and she sailed south with Skipper George Downs and 25 crew. Although more than half the time was spent in port for repairs, at times Boston Lincoln found shoals of hake so thick she could have caught 200-300 tonnes a day. On hearing this the Argentinian government promptly declared a 100 mile fishing limit. She returned with Skipper Stan Taylor in command in March 1973. As a result it was felt that for future fishing on these grounds larger factory ships, with bigger crews

would be needed.

Boston Lincoln after a spell as a Trinity House Guard vessel was sold in 1985, the last of the 5 Boston D.S.F. large Freezer stern trawlers to be sold. She was converted for standby work.

Now Maria De Lurdes Viepra - Panama registered standby safety vessel.

X Milu Vierira 1985.
X Boston Lincoln 1985.

BOSTON YORK

From the 1960's Poland, in an effort to attract much needed foreign currency, began to build bargain price ships. Many countries took up the opportunity to build up their fleets including fishing companies of which Boston D.S.F. was one.

Name	Reg. No.	Off. No.	Tons	Length/ Breadth	Call Sign
Boston York	H 3	334087	846 285	212.0 38.4	GYBH

Builder	Type
Stocznia Im Komuny Paraskiej	Wholefish Freezer

Factory Details

21,200 cu.ft. fish hold
5 Jackstone Froster V.P. Freezers
5 x 20 Station freezers capable of freezing 30 tons per day

Engine Details

Mirrlees National Ltd.
Type KLSSMR 8
2500 BHP   15½ knots

Launched	Skipper Maiden Voyage	Crew No.
31st January 1968	George Downs	22-28

Named by

Izabella Greczanik, a journalist with the local newspaper Gós Wybrzeia

Boston York was laid down on the 11th September 1967 designated Class B427/A4. She was the first All Freezer trawler built by Poland for British owners, the smallest of four similar design ships. She arrived in Hull on the 5th July 1968. On her way from Poland she had problems with her engines overheating, but her chief engineer fathomed out the problem during her maiden voyage. It was due to sand being left in the engine water cooler pipes, while they were being shaped at the shipyard. This was causing a blockage and overheating of the engine.

Boston York sailed from Hull on the 18th July 1968 commanded by Skipper George Downs and after a 32 day trip to the White Sea grounds landed back in Hull with 350 tonnes of frozen whole fish, which was almost a capacity catch, her fish hold being able to hold 350-400 tonnes depending on stowage. During 1969 Boston York landed a total of 2,790 tonnes of frozen fish.

A sad fact of life on trawlers was sabotage by disillusioned crew members, varying from dumping crockery, to tampering with steering gear and fires. In September 1971 whilst outward bound to the fishing grounds, a crew member lit 4 fires. These were detected by the ship's fire detection system. Skipper Ray Richardson took the Boston York into Aberdeen and the police removed the crewman responsible.

In February 1973 Boston York was chartered by Canadian interests to fish off Labrador, with Skipper Jimmy Chayter. This proved a success and Boston York was sold to the Canadians later in the year and was renamed Zarag-

oza, based at St. Johns, Newfoundland. On the 17th October 1983, after being on fire off Catalina, Newfoundland she capsized and sank.

Zaragoza lost 1983
X Boston York 1973

LADY PARKES

Name	Reg. No.	Off. No.	Tons	Length/ Breadth	Call Sign
Lady Parkes	H 397	308543	1746	240.3	GSKH
			690	41.1	

Builder	Type
Hall Russell & Co. Ltd. Aberdeen 1966	Wholefish Freezer

Factory Details

27,000 cu.ft. fish hold
11 x 12 Station Jackstone Froster V.P. Freezers
Later 13 x 12 Station Freezers after filleting lines removed
Baader fillet processing line.

Engine Details

Mirrlees National Ltd.
Type KLSSMR MK 2
2350 BHP 13½ knots

Launched	Skipper Maiden Voyage	Crew No.
22nd February 1966	Peter Craven	24-31

Named by
Mrs J. Ingle, grand-daughter of Sir Fred Parkes

Lady Parkes sailed directly from Aberdeen to the N. E. Canadian fishing grounds on the 18th May 1966, commanded by Skipper Peter Craven on her maiden voyage. Fishing was slack at the Newfoundland and Labrador grounds and the Lady Parkes steamed an estimated 12,000 miles in 68 days, to bring home a capacity catch of 543 tonnes of cod and codling. She arrived at her home port of Hull for the first time on the 25th July 1966. Her catch was the first to be unloaded by automatic conveyor belt system.

Leaving Hull on the 4th August for her 2nd voyage the Lady Parkes returned to the N.E. Atlantic grounds (Labrador and Greenland) and whilst moving among ice, sustained damage below the water line. The water tight bulkhead system and pumps stopped any severe flooding and she arrived back at Hull on the 8th October 1966 after a 67 day trip to land 502 tonnes of wholefish and 15 tonnes of fillets. After repairs in dry dock she sailed on the 29th October.

In 1968 Lady Parkes was the top British Freezer, landing 3,790 tonnes.

In 1969 Lady Parkes had the distinction of being the only trawler to be mentioned in the Guinness Book of Records for landing a record 4,169 tonnes of fish in 7 trips in 288 days at sea, commanded by Skipper Peter Craven on 6 trips and Skipper Paddy Donoghue on 1 trip. Again she was the top British Freezer.

On the 11th June 1977 the fishing community was surprised to learn that Lady Parkes had been sold to French owners for conversion to a research vessel. Her new role is working in the French Antarctic as a geophysical, seismographic research vessel for shore installations.

Now Odyssee
X Odys Echo 1987
X Resolution 1985
X Lady Parkes 1977

PRINCESS ANNE

Princess Anne was the first British built trawler, constructed to Lloyd's Class 1 ice specification. Her hull had extra thick plating and closer frame spacing. This meant she could fish in the ice fields of the far north. Gregson and Co. Ltd. ran into financial difficulties and the Clelands Shipbuilders were responsible for her completion.

Princess Anne, commanded by Skipper Peter Craven, sailed on her maiden voyage from Hull on the 8th October 1974 and from a very good 32 day trip to the White Sea landed 664 tonnes of mainly big cod. On her 3rd trip a 53 day trip to the White Sea on which it snowed nearly every day she set up another record catch of 779 tonnes.

In December 1975 Princess Anne was steaming home

Name	Reg. No.	Off. No.	Tons	Length/ Breadth	Call Sign
Princess Anne	H 269	362252	1476 541	251.3 42.0	GTHL

Builder	Type
Gregson and Co. Ltd (Blyth) and Clelands S.B. Co. Ltd. Wallsend 1974	Wholefish Freezer

Factory Details

800 ton capacity fish hold
2 banks of 8 x 12 Station Jackstone Froster V.P. Freezers able to freeze 50 tons per day.
650 cu.ft. halibut room
Baader type 166 gutting machine

Engine Details

Mirrlees Blackstone
2x Type KLSSMR 2
2 x 1800 BHP 16 knots

Launched	Skipper Maiden Voyage	Crew No.
15th May 1973	Peter Craven	21-27

Named by

Mrs Jess Webb, wife of Mr Kenneth Webb Chairman of Birds Eye Foods Ltd.

with a good catch from the Newfoundland grounds, with the crew looking forward to some Christmas leave. Soon after leaving the grounds a severe gale blew up, from which she was lucky to survive. She was steaming full speed in a severe following sea with the wind well abaft of the beam,

which would keep her catch in good condition for many months.

After her last trip from landing mackerel in Holland, Princess Anne with Skipper Craven sailed from Hull on the 13th November 1981 to Bergen, Norway, to be converted to a survey ship. She was sold due to lack of all year round fishing grounds, another victim of small quotas.

Now Polar Prince, Canadian seismographic survey ship. X Princess Anne 1981

when she dropped off the top of a big wave down into a deep trough. The impact put one engine immediately out of action with a fractured sea water pipe, but the other engine kept going. One of the engineers described this effect as like dropping down in a very fast lift, then being hurled off one's feet by the impact which blacked out the ship and displaced many of the engine room gratings. Princess Anne was undoubtedly saved because of her very strong construction. Also the fact that she had two main engines allowed her to maintain power and mobility.

Although Princess Anne had bent some plates, after light repairs in St. Johns she came back home docking on Christmas Day 1975.

Princess Anne was one of the ships chosen to represent the fishing fleet, at the Queen's Jubilee Review of the Fleet at Spithead on the 28th June 1977. She came straight from the fishing grounds to Hull for stores, then down to Spithead for 5 days and unloaded her catch after the event. She was able to do this due to the excellent cold store plant

SIR FRED PARKES

The Sir Fred Parkes was Boston Deep Sea Fisheries first freezer stern trawler and was named after the founder of the company. After running fishing trials off the Scottish coast, commanded by Skipper Bernard Wharam, she sailed from Stornaway on the 12th March 1966 direct to the Labrador and Newfoundland fishing grounds for her maiden voyage. She steamed an estimated 8,000 miles during a 56 day trip arriving at her home port of Hull on the 7th May 1966, landing 516 tonnes of fish. The Sir Fred Parkes was put on public display and a reception party was held for visiting dignitaries. Her chief engineer was Harry Skoyles and mate Jack Curtis.

The Sir Fred Parkes and her sister Lady Parkes were built with Baader fillet lines, the intention being that during slack fishing the hands could work this line. For instance from her 3rd voyage she landed 585 tonnes of wholefish and 30 tonnes of fillets. But after only a short working life the fillet lines were removed.

Name	Reg. No.	Off. No.	Tons	Length/Breadth	Call Sign
Sir Fred Parkes	H 385	308533	1737	240.3	GSDE
			706	41.1	

Builder	Type
Hall Russell & Co. Ltd. Aberdeen 1966	Wholefish Freezer

Factory Details

27,000 cu.ft. fish hold
11 x 12 Station Jackstone Froster V.P. Freezers
Later 13 x 12 Station Freezers after filleting line removed
Baader fillet processing line
570 tons capacity

Engine Details

Mirrlees National Ltd.
Type KLSSMR MK 2
2350 BHP 13½ knots

Launched	Skipper Maiden Voyage	Crew No.
9th December 1965	Bernard Wharam	24-31

Named by

Mrs M. Snelling daughter of Sir Basil Parkes, granddaughter of Sir Fred Parkes

On the 22nd May 1968 whilst the Sir Fred Parkes was discharging her catch of 568 tonnes at Hull's fish dock a fire broke out in the officer's saloon which rapidly spread, and soon a large fire was sweeping through the accommodation. Men working on board rapidly evacuated the ship, but one man was trapped by the smoke in the chief engineer's cabin.

Fortunately the Hull Fire Brigade were swiftly at the scene and a hole was cut in the superstructure and he was pulled free, unharmed. It was the first major fire where foam was used at a cost of £200 — a small price to pay for saving a trawler worth almost half a million pounds.

After the fire had been extinguished unloading of the catch was resumed and on completion repairs were begun by Humber St Andrews Engineering Company which lasted until the 10th September 1968 when she was fit for sea again.

In December 1972 the Sir Fred Parkes, after bunkering at Vardo, Norway, split her keel on an underwater obstruction. She was towed to Harstad for repairs, but it was decided to bring her home. During the tow home severe gales occurred and this caused concern for her safety. But the large Norwegian tug and the Sir Fred Parkes weathered the storm and arrived safely in Hull.

In September 1973 whilst fishing between Bear Island and Spitzbergen a fire broke out in the net hold destroying all but 2 nets, so she had to go into Honningsvaag for new nets.

Despite her problems the Sir Fred Parkes landed plenty of good trips in her time, regularly landing 500 - 600 tonnes. In 1969 her total catch was 3,443 tonnes.

On the 22nd April 1982, the Sir Fred Parkes fishing role ended and she joined the growing number of trawlers working as stand by ships for the oil industry. Her new owners were Putford Enterprises Ltd., business associates of the Boston Group.

In 1987 the Sir Fred Parkes was bought by S.F.P. Atlantic Fisheries Ltd. for returning to fishing and was re-registered at Hull as H39 and renamed Waveney Warrior.

BOYD LINE LTD.

Boyd Line was founded in 1936 by Thomas Boyd who had long family connections with the fishing industry. He was Manager of Thomas Hamlings for 39 years, before forming his own company. In 1937 he started with 3 new distant-water trawlers and by 1939 the fleet had grown to 6 ships. They were taken into Naval Service during the Second World War.

After the war the founder's son, Thomas W. Boyd D.S.O., returned from a distinguished war service in the R.N.V.R. to become Managing Director of Boyd Line in 1950, and also Managing Director of Lord Line.

In 1963 he left Lord Line to concentrate on running Boyd Line, which had become a good size family fishing company, having overseen the building of Associated Fisheries' stern trawler the "Lord Nelson". Having recognised the

Preparing the "Otago Buccaneer" for New Zealand are Dolphin Bowl winning Skippers (left to right) Terry Thresh, George Kent and Mate Tony Tuton.

potential. Thomas W. Boyd ordered Boyd Line's first freezer in 1964 which was followed by 4 Polish built vessels including the sister ships, Arctic Buccaneer and Arctic Galliard, which from 1976 became the top British Trawlers.

A NEW FUTURE FOR ARCTIC BUCCANEER AND ARCTIC GALLIARD

By the 1980's, with the loss of the freedom to fish the traditional grounds of North East Canada, Greenland,

43

Mrs. T.W. Boyd being presented with the traditional bouquet by the shipyard's youngest apprentice before launching the "Arctic Freebooter". Photo by courtesy of Boyd Line.

Iceland, Norwegian waters and the White Sea, combined with cheap white fish imports, most freezers were being sold out of fishing, for conversion into oil industry vessels.

Boyd Line however, on the sale of the Arctic Buccaneer and sister ship Arctic Galliard to Fletcher Fishing Ltd. of Dunedin, New Zealand, were able to secure jobs for their skippers and crews, whose expertise in deep sea trawling would help make a success of the new venture in New Zealand.

In early 1982 the ships were renamed Otago Buccaneer and Otago Galliard, the prefix being the county in which Dunedin is situated. Also they were given a new livery - blue hull with yellow line, white funnel with a red heraldic lion's head and a black top. Otago Buccaneer's fishing No. became 7939 and Otago Galliard No.7940.

The Otago Buccaneer and Otago Galliard began fishing in New Zealand waters in May 1982. They fish all the Islands waters, except to the north, for orange roughy, hoki, hake, warehou, oreo-dory and squid, trawling in depths as great as 1,000 metres.

In the last 6 years, the 2 ships have become the most successful trawlers fishing from New Zealand. They have landed 880 ton capacity catches of processed orange roughy equal to 1.4 million fish. This high value fish has dramatically increased New Zealand's fish exports income.

Hull skippers and some crew are still flying out to Dunedin for 4 month tours of duty but the majority have now settled in Dunedin and the Port now has its own "Hessle Road". They are now training a new generation of local deep sea fishermen to carry on in the years to come.

During the decline of the fishing industry in the 1980's Boyd Line, along with many other old established trawler

The "Arctic Galliard" being launched at Gdynia. Photo by courtesy of Boyd Line.

owners, began a desperate battle to keep fishing. Some of the fleet had to be sold, but in 1986 a gamble to send the "Arctic Corsair" back fishing paid off and since then 2 freezer stern trawlers have been acquired for the fleet. Boyd Line also runs a Management Services company.

Thomas Boyd, the founder's grandson, is the present Chairman, having succeeded his father in 1982. He joined Boyd Line in 1962.

NAMES: Arctic Prefix.
FUNNEL: Black top, white with 2 red bands.
HULL: Black with red line.

ARCTIC BUCCANEER

Arctic Buccaneer arrived in Hull from the Polish building yard on the 6th December with Skipper Terry Thresh. Due to being built overseas and also the biggest trawler to join the British Fleet, her arrival caused great interest to the media and local public. To please the many waiting photographers a high speed run down to St Andrew's Docks was arranged. On arriving opposite the dock she turned to go back to Albert Dock back down the river, but suddenly her variable pitch propeller went out of control and she charged towards the landing stage, straight at the sidewinder Arctic Vandal which was waiting to enter the locks. Skipper Thresh stopped the engines and ordered the anchor to be dropped. Thankfully she was brought to a stop and a tragedy was averted.

Shortly after arriving in Hull, it was found that Arctic Buccaneer was suffering from excessive axial propeller vibration and she had to return to the builder's yard for

Name	Reg. No.	Off. No.	Tons	Length/ Breadth	Call Sign
Arctic Buccaneer	H 188	362201	1660	280.6	GTEN
			793	42.9	

Builder	Type
Stocznia Im Komuny Paraskiej Gdynia 1973	Wholefish Freezer

Factory Details
40,500 cu.ft. fish hold
16 x 12 Station Jackstone Froster V P Freezers
Capable of freezing 60 tons per day
2 x Baader 424 headers (1982)

Engine Details
Zgoda Sultzer
Type 8 ZBH 40/80 8 Cyl
4800 BHP 15½ knots

Launched	Skipper Maiden Voyage	Crew No.
31st March 1973	Richard Sackville-Bryant	24-33

Named by
Mrs Elizabeth Boyd, wife of Mr. Thomas Boyd Director of Boyd Line.

alterations. Unfortunately this cost her a full year's fishing and it wasn't until February 1975 that she arrived back in Hull along with her sister ship.

Arctic Buccaneer sailed on her maiden voyage on the 17th April commanded by Skipper Dicky Bryant who took her to the White Sea grounds, returning after 70 days to Hull. Her trip of 724 tonnes took from 29th May till 3rd

Photo by courtesy of Walter Fussey & Son.

June. The catch consisted of 676 tonnes cod, 32 haddock, 2 plaice, 3½ cats, 3½ coalfish and 5 tonnes mixed.

During the next 7 years Arctic Buccaneer became one of Hull's most successful trawlers as can be seen from the Dolphin Bowl Charts which she won in 1978 with Skipper Stan Barwick and in 1979 with Skipper George Kent.

On the 14th October with only small whitefish quotas available, Arctic Buccaneer sailed to Bremerhaven to be adapted for mackerel fishing in home waters which was to become her role until the end of 1981. She was sold to Fletcher Fishing Co. of Dunedin, New Zealand on the 18th January, sailing from Hull on the 18th April 1982 with Skipper Michael Landrick and a Hull crew.

Now Otago Buccaneer
X Arctic Buccaneer 1982.

ARCTIC FREEBOOTER

Name	Reg. No.	Off. No.	Tons	Length/ Breadth	Call Sign
Arctic Freebooter	H 362	308527	1633	242.7	GRLV
			693	41.0	

Builder	Type
Goole Shipbuilding & Eng. Co. Goole 1966	Wholefish Freezer

Factory Details

28,250 cu.ft. fish hold
10 x 12 Station Jackstone Froster vertical plate freezers capable of freezing 40 tons per day in 100lb blocks

Engine Details

Mirrlees National Ltd.
Monarch ALSSM 6
2380 BHP 15½ knots

Launched	Skipper Maiden Voyage	Crew No.
3rd May 1965	Richard Sackville-Bryant	26

Named by

Mrs Barbara Boyd, wife of Mr.T.W. Boyd D.S.O.,O.B.E., Chairman & Managing Director of Boyd Line

Arctic Freebooter was Boyd Line's first freezer and also the first built at Goole. After her launch she took a list to starboard and during her fitting out, severe fires broke out on two occasions, which delayed her completion. But any misgivings anyone had were soon dispelled and over the years Arctic Freebooter has been a most popular and successful ship.

She sailed from Hull on her maiden voyage on the 16th February 1966, commanded by Skipper Dicky Bryant who took her to the Newfoundland grounds. After 53 days she landed at Hull with 479 tonnes, mainly of cod.

In March 1965 after a 53 day trip to the Norwegian coast, Skipper Bryant landed a record catch of haddock of around 500 tonnes in 8,100 blocks and also 2,200 blocks of cod. In 1969 Arctic Freebooter was Boyd Line's top ship, landing 3,440 tonnes from 301 days at sea.

In 1975 she won the Dolphin Bowl for the previous year's catch which totalled over 3,400 tonnes, including 2,221 tonnes of cod and 979 tonnes of haddock. Skipper George Kent was in command for 6 trips and Skipper R.S. Bryant 1 trip. Arctic Freebooter spent 306 days at sea, doing 2 trips to the Norwegian coast and 5 to the White Sea.

In 1985 Arctic Freebooter was converted to standby

work and was chartered by the Royal Navy. On the 9th July she was sold to Stanley, Witte, Boyd, a joint venture by Falklands, Swedish and Boyd Line interests, to fish the Falklands

After a refit in Hull she was renamed Lord Shackleton on the 28th September. She sailed for the Falkland Islands on the 1st December 1987 with a Hull crew.

Now Lord Shackleton
X Arctic Freebooter 1987.

ARCTIC GALLIARD

Built in Poland to Lloyd's Class + 100A1, Arctic Galliard and Buccaneer were strengthened to Lloyd's Ice Class 2, which meant they could have 100 tonnes of ice on their upper deck and superstructure along with 90 tonnes of fish on the factory deck and still be above international stability requirements.

When Arctic Galliard ran her trials in the Baltic in March 1974 she was found to have the same problem as her sister ship, excessive axial propeller vibration. She was kept at the builder's yard until Feb 1975. Arctic Galliard and her sister Arctic Buccaneer were the biggest British trawlers built, equipped with a vast factory deck and powerful engines.

On the 21st May 1975 Arctic Galliard, commanded by Skipper Terry Thresh, sailed on her maiden voyage to the grounds east of Vardo and Cape Kanin. On her return in August after 66 days she landed 845 tonnes in 16,296 blocks. This consisted of 2,556 cod, 11,756 codling, 1016

Name	Reg. No.	Off. No.	Tons	Length/ Breadth	Call Sign
Arctic Galliard	H 195	362209	1660	280.6	GTEP
			793	42.9	

Builder	Type
Stocznia Im Komuny Paraskiej Gdynia 1973 (Class B 420)	Wholefish Freezer

Factory Details

40,500 cu.ft. Fish hold
16 x 12 Station Jackstone Froster V.P. Freezers
capable of freezing 60 tons per day

Engine Details

Zgoda Sulzer
Type 8ZBH 40/80 cyl
4800 BHP 15½ knots

Launched	Skipper Maiden Voyage	Crew No.
10th May 1973	Terry Thresh	24-33

Named by

Mrs Ann Martin, daughter of Mr. T.W. Boyd D.S.O. O.B.E., Chairman & Managing Director of Boyd Line

Photo by courtesy of Boyd Line.

haddock, 240 catfish, 30 mock-halibut, 2 reds, 17 saithe and 691 flatfish.

Arctic Galliard went on to win the Dolphin Bowl Trophy in 1976 and 1977, commanded by Skipper T. Thresh, Ch. Eng. R.T. Sellers and mate Fred Nottingham.

In 1982 with no reasonable white fish quotas available, and mackerel prices at rock bottom, the Arctic Galliard was sold to Fletcher Fishing Company New Zealand, sail-ing from Hull on the 21st March 1982 commanded by Skipper George Kent. Although she had been highly successful in her 7 years fishing northern waters, like the Otago Galliard she is still providing work for Hull crews who fly out to New Zealand to fish the southern waters.

1976 DOLPHIN BOWL

WHITE SEA AND N. COAST
59 days   818 tons   11 April

WHITE SEA, BEAR ISLAND
52 days   850 tons   21 June (New Record)
78 days   836 tons   21 Sept*

49

HOME WATERS

24 days	845 tons	22 Nov
20 days	862 tons	24 Dec

All trips were with Terry Thresh except * Chris Hamling. The last trip of 862 tons was a new British Record.

ARCTIC PRIVATEER

Arctic Privateer arrived in Hull from her Polish builder's yard on the 10th September 1968. She was the same design as the Boston York, but 16' longer. On the 19th September she sailed from Hull on her maiden voyage commanded by Skipper Paddy Boyle and after a 58 day trip to the White Sea grounds landed 7.128 kits of frozen fish (445.5 tonnes), consisting of 6154 kits cod, 944 kits haddock and 30 kits of mixed. Her Chief Engineer was Albert Wallace and her mate Joe Jefferson. During 1969 her daily average was 11.18 tonnes.

Arctic Privateer, like her sister ship, was popular with crews mainly because of the good fish handling equipment.

In 1974 the Ministry of Agriculture, Fishery and Food needed to replace the 20 year old Fishery research ship, Sir William Hardy. They required a bigger ship for deep water research into handling, storing and processing at sea, and in March 1974 they acquired the Arctic Privateer from Boyd Line. The work to convert her into a research ship took 18 months and on completion she became the Ministry's fourth research ship. She was renamed G.A. Reay, after the first director of the Torry Fishery Research Station at Aberdeen and her new number was A147. She carried 23

Name	Reg. No.	Off. No.	Tons	Length/ Breadth	Call Sign
Arctic Privateer	H 441	344098	928	228.1	GYMA
			322	39.8	

Builder	Type
Stocznia Im Komuny Paraskiej Gdynia 1968	Wholefish Freezer

Factory Details

26,000 cu.ft. fish hold
2 Rows of 6 Jackstone Froster V.P. Freezers capable of freezing 37.5 tons per day.

Engine Details

Mirrlees National Ltd.
Type KLSSMR 8
2500 BHP 14½ knots

Launched	Skipper Maiden Voyage	Crew No.
2nd April 1968	Bill (Paddy) Boyle	25

Named by

Mrs Barbara Boyd, wife of Mr. T. W. Boyd O.B.E., D.S.O., Chairman & Managing Director of Boyd Line.

crew and 6 scientists. On the 4th July 1984 the G.A. Reay was bought by J. Marr & Sons to join their scientific research fleet and in 1985 her role was changed to oceanographic research.

In December 1986 G.A. Reay was given a refit and on being chartered to the Falkland Islands Government as a fishery patrol ship was renamed Falklands Right. She sailed from Hull in February 1987 and on her return late in the year her name was changed again to Eastella.

Now Eastella Oceanographic Research Vessel
X Falklands Right 1987
X G.A. Reay 1987
X Arctic Privateer 1976

ARCTIC RAIDER

When Arctic Raider arrived at her home port of Hull on the 23rd December, she brought the port's number of stern trawlers to 20. She sailed on her maiden voyage on the 11th February 1969. Skipper Terry Thresh fished the White Sea and Norwegian coast grounds, arriving back home on the 2nd March 1969, landing 441 tonnes, made up of 356 tonnes of cod, 73 tonnes haddock, 8 tonnes halibut and 4 tonnes mixed fish. The Chief Engineer for this voyage was Ernie Lewis and the mate Fred Nottingham. Like her sister ship she was popular with crews. In 1969 her daily average

Name	Reg. No.	Off. No.	Tons	Length/ Breadth	Call Sign
Arctic Raider	H 440	334103	928	228.1	GYLZ
			322	39.8	

Builder	Type
Stocznia Im Komuny Paraskiej Gdynia 1968	Wholefish Freezer

Factory Details
26,000 cu.ft. fish hold 2 rows of 6 Jackstone Froster V.P. Freezers able to freeze 37.5 tons per day

Engine Details
Mirrlees National Ltd. Type KLSSMR 8 2500 BHP 14½ knots

Launched	Skipper Maiden Voyage	Crew No.
31st July 1968	Terry Thresh	25

Named by
Mrs Elizabeth Eastwood, daughter of Mr. T.W. Boyd, D.S.O.,O.B.E., Chairman & Managing Director of Boyd Line

was 11.71 tonnes and on occasions in the 1970's she was one of the top 20 British freezers by weight of fish caught.

At 4 a.m. on the 3rd December 1975, whilst outward bound for Spitzbergen, the Arctic Raider had the sad distinction of being the last trawler to leave the St Andrew's fish dock. She left behind a dock empty of trawlers for the first time in 92 years.

Photo by courtesy of Boyd Line.

In the 1980's with their fishing role uneconomic, most trawlers were being used as stand-by vessels for the oil industry. Arctic Raider became a Trinity House guard vessel between 1983/4, then she was sold to Iranian owners. With a Korean crew she sailed from Hull for the Indian Ocean on the 31st December 1984.

Now Hamoor 2 Iranian Owners
X Arctic Raider 1984

BRITISH UNITED TRAWLERS

British United Trawlers was formed on the 1st July 1969 when Associated Fisheries merged with the Ross Group. The Company took over a fleet of 120 trawlers, including 13 large freezer stern trawlers under the management of a number of subsidiary companies in most of Britain's fishing ports. The Board was made up of Bernard Boxall (Chairman), Graham Hellyer (Managing Director), Bill Letten (Dept. Managing Director), Michael Noble (Chairman Associated Fisheries), Alexander S. Alexander (Chairman Ross Group), Mr. A. Barrowman, Mr. A.M. Davies, Mark Hellyer, Mr. E. Waller and Mr. C.B. Zealley.

The Company enjoyed many successes during the 1970's but from 1975 the sidewinder fleet began being scrapped due to the loss of the Icelandic grounds, and in the 1980's with the quotas hitting the freezers, 3 were scrapped and by 1986 the rest sold to foreign owners.

The Company had many liveries for their ships under various subsidiaries. British United Trawlers' own livery was:-

NAME THEME: Ancient Tribes
FUNNEL: White with B.U.T. logo
HULL: Blue

The "Kelt" was one of many trawlers to join British United Trawlers' fleet. Photo by courtesy of Walter Fussey & Son.

THE FREEEZER FLEET
ASSOCIATED FISHERIES

Hellyer Bros
Cassio
Coriolanus
Lord Nelson
Orsino
Othello

Northern Trawlers
Conqueror
Defiance
Victory

ROSS GROUP

Ross Group Hull
Ross Illustrious
Ross Implacable
Ross Intrepid
Invincible

Ross Group Grimsby
Ross Valiant
Ross Vanguard

B.U.T. BUILT FREEZERS

From 1972, 5 new freezers built for B.U.T. joined the fleet. For a name theme it was decided to use the Hellyer pre-war theme of Ancient tribes.

HULL	GRIMSBY
Dane	Goth
Norse	Roman
Pict	

THE RANGER FLEET (1973)

Ranger Apollo	became	Turcoman
Ranger Aurora	"	Esquimaux
Ranger Boreas	"	Afghan
Ranger Brisies	"	Hausa
Ranger Cadmus	"	Arab
Ranger Calliope	"	Kelt
Ranger Callisto	"	Kuro
Ranger Castor	"	Gaul

DANE

Delivered in March 1973 the Dane, and then her sister Pict, were built with roll reduction tanks and deep bilge keels; Also with greater use of incombustible materials, sprinkler and fire detection systems, fire proof doors and bulkheads. Due to the large amount of offal created on factory ships a fish meal plant was installed and a large storage hold.

Name	Reg. No.	Off. No.	Tons	Length/Breadth	Call Sign
Dane	H 144	359160	1480	243.0	GQHR
			485	42.2	

Builder	Type
Brooke Marine Ltd.	Factory
Lowestoft 1973	Freezer

Factory Details	Baader Equipment
18,700 cu.ft. fish hold	Type 412 Headers
Jacksone Froster H.P. Freezers	Type 613 Gutters
able to freeze 24 tons of fillets	Type 99 Filleters
per day in 7 or 14lb packs	Type 188 Filleters
Fish meal hold 11264 cu.ft.	Type 47 Skinners
Liver oil 41 tons	
Fish oil residue 32 tons	

Engine Details

Mirrlees Blackstone Ltd.
Type KMR 7 Major
3246 BHP 13½ knots

Launched	Skipper Maiden Voyage	Crew No.
16th May 1972	Roy Waller	35

Named by

Mrs J.M.L. Prior, wife of the Minister of A.F. & F.

Dane sailed on her maiden voyage from Hull on the 2nd March 1973 commanded by Skipper Roy Waller who took her fishing to the Norwegian Coast and White Sea Grounds. Dane was so successful in her first year she was Champion British Trawler and winner of the 1974 Dolphin Bowl Trophy. With skippers Roy Waller and Charles Thresh she caught an estimated 2,911.3 tonnes, but factory freezer skippers felt that they caught much more fish to turn into fillets than they were credited with.

But even Champion Trawlers faced setbacks. Just after Christmas 1977 after a few hauls at the beginning of a trip to Spitzbergen Dane's electric winch motor burnt out and she had to return home to Hull for repairs. On 29th November 1975 after returning from a trip to Murmansk Dane was put on display for the public during Hull City Council's civic week.

In October 1977 Dane, commanded by skipper Jack Lilley, was the first trawler to have a bar fitted in her crew mess room where off-duty crewmen were allowed 2 pints a day while stocks lasted, costing 15p per pint of lager or bitter. This experiment requested by the Department of Trade was designed to combat illegal drinking on trawlers. By tradition sidewinder crews took a case of beer and a bottle of spirits away to combat the misery of the first few

days back at sea. Most owners fought this practice because of the likelihood of accidents. The only exception was strike breaking crews, and then a blind eye was turned.

In 1984 when only 11 years old, but with no quotas for fish, B.U.T. had to sell the Dane. She was converted into a geophysical research vessel and now sails under the Panamanian flag.

Now Western Caribbean Research Vessel
X Anvil Cross 1984
X Dane 1984

GOTH

The Goth and her 2 sister trawlers were designed by B.U.T.'s Norwegian Naval Architect, Mr. J.A. Tvedt.

After running her trials in Scottish waters Goth came to her home port of Grimsby and sailed on her maiden voyage in the early hours of the 20th February 1974, commanded by Skipper Jack N. Kerr who took Goth to the North East Arctic grounds. The trawler encountered the usual technical problems, one of the major ones being problems with flushing offal from the factory deck which was causing flooding. Despite this a very good catch of 618 tonnes was landed after a 56 day trip.

In December 1975 Goth towed the disabled Ross Implacable from Honningsvaag home, through the south Fjords arriving at Grimsby on the 17th December. This was a long tow of about 1300 miles.

From the mid 1970's Canada and Norway became worried about the drastic reduction of fish stocks in their home waters, due mainly to large fleets of factory trawlers (some

Name	Reg. No.	Off. No.	Tons	Length/ Breadth	Call Sign
Goth	GY 252	357897	1448	207.0	GUDS
			536	41.1	

Builder	Type
Ferguson Bros (Pt Glas) Ltd.	Wholefish
Port Glasgow 1974	Freezer

Factory Details

30,000 cu.ft. fish hold
6 x 20 Station Jackstone Froster V.P. freezers
Capable of freezing 37.5 tons per day
120 42" x 21" x 4" blocks every 3 hrs 20 mins.

Engine Details

Mirrlees Blackstone Ltd.
Type K Major 6
3180 BHP 13½ knots

Launched	Skipper Maiden Voyage	Crew No.
28th June 1973	Jack Noble Kerr	24

Named by

Mrs J.B. Godber, wife of the Minister of Ag. Food and Fish.

of which could catch 2,000 baskets in one haul) constantly fishing the grounds, and a system of quotas and units was imposed.

This greatly affected the British Freezer fleets' fishing opportunities, and to keep the ships employed in all year round fishing, owners sent their freezers to fish home waters, for herring and mackerel fishing:- September—November, West Scotland waters; November - March, Cornish waters; then on to White Fish as quotas would allow.

During 1978, in an attempt to find other work B.U.T. discussed Greenland shrimp fishing with Faroese Skipper Johan Plogv who had acquired the Ross Valiant for shrimping. Acting on his advice the Goth was equipped with Norwegian shrimp nets and obtained a licence from the International Commission for North Atlantic Fisheries to catch 475 tonnes of shrimps at West Greenland, issued by the British Government. Goth left Grimsby on the 3rd June 1978 for West Greenland and then 36 hours after she began fishing and had caught 11 tonnes of top quality shrimps, a Danish Fishery Protection vessel came alongside and ordered Goth to leave the grounds as she was illegally fishing. After diplomatic discussions it transpired that Britain was the only EEC country not granted quotas to fish at West Greenland. The Goth was arrested and fined but as she was felt to be the victim of fishing bureaucracy she was

allowed to keep her fishing gear, which is usually confiscated. As Goth returned home she tried shrimp fishing off East Scotland but the trip ended as a commercial failure. This was in no way due to any fault of the owners, the Goth or her crew. On the 10th September 1978 B.U.T. transferred Goth from Grimsby to Hull with her regular Skipper Jack Kerr and his crew - a sad time for a Skipper who pioneered freezer trawling out of Grimsby over 14 years earlier. The port was now left without any freezers. In 1981 Goth was withdrawn from regular fishing and spent many months laid up at Hull, until her sale to Norwegian owners in 1984.

Now Ocean Trawler
X Jan Mayen 1987
X Goth 1984

NORSE

The Norse ran her trials at Loch Fyne and had a week's fishing trials off Fair Isle. The catch of big coley and hake was sold for charity. In March 1974 for her maiden voyage Skipper Roy Waller took Norse to the White Sea grounds and on her return to Hull after 56 days she landed 560 tonnes. On her 3rd trip with her fishroom crammed full she landed 660 tonnes.

On her next trip Norse took a film crew to make a film about fishing and tried her luck on the Canadian grounds. But the only fish to be found were swaddies (redfish), so she worked south and ended up on St. George's Bank, 150 miles from New York. Here she caught 70 tonnes of haddock in 5 days and much to the delight of the crew plenty of

Name	Reg. No.	Off. No.	Tons	Length/ Breadth	Call Sign
Norse	H 193	362217	1448 537	210.0 41.1	GUDT

Builder	Type
Scott and Son (Bowling) Ltd. Bowling 1974	Wholefish Freezer

Factory Details

30,000 cu.ft. fish hold
6 x 20 Station Jacksone Froster V.P. Freezers
Each of the 6 able to freeze 2,000lb fish in 42" x 21" x 4"
blocks in 3 hrs 20 mins or 37.5 tonnes per day

Engine Details

Mirrlees Blackstone
Type K Major 6
3180 BHP 13½ knots

Launched	Skipper Maiden Voyage	Crew No.
16th August 1973	Roy Waller	29

Named by

Mrs P.M. Tapscott, wife of the Chairman of B.U.T.

Photo by courtesy of Walter Fussey & Son.

lobsters. On her return to Hull Norse landed 450 tonnes, 300 tonnes of which were reds mainly for the continental markets.

Norse won the Dolphin Bowl for 1975. Skipper Roy Waller made 4 of the 5 trips and Skipper Roger Pepper one. Norse caught 3,094 tonnes of fish from the N.E. Arctic grounds of White Sea, Bear Island and Norwegian coast.

This was a creditable performance due to the limited quotas available to the large B.U.T. fleet. She was runner up in 1976.

A Previous Norse owned by Hellyer Bros. was H 219 built at Beverley in 1925. Of 394 tonnes and 147' long, she was wrecked at Iceland on the 6th March 1929. Her crew of 19 were all rescued.

Now Northern Osprey, fishing for Canadian owners.
X Osprey 1987
X Norse 1984

PICT

Name	Reg. No.	Off. No.	Tons	Length/Breadth	Call Sign
Pict	H 150	359184	1478	230.0	GQHS
			495	42.3	

Builder	Type
Brooke Marine Ltd.	Factory
Lowestoft 1973	Freezer

Factory Details	Baader Equipment
18,770 cu.ft. fish holds	Type 412 Headers
Jackstone Froster H.P. Freezer	Type 613 Gutters
Capable of freezing 24 tons	Type 99 Filleters
of fillets a day. 7 or 14lb packs	Type 188 Filleters
Fish meal hold 11,264 cu.ft.	Type 47 Skinners
Liver oil 41 tons	
Fish oil residue 21 tons	

Engine Details

Mirrlees Blackstone Ltd.
Type KMR7 Major
3246 BHP 13½ knots

Launched	Skipper Maiden Voyage	Crew No.
22nd November 1972	Joe Russell	35

Named by

Mrs A.S. Alexander, wife of the Deputy Chairman of B.U.T.

Pict, like her sister trawler Dane, was the largest of the Humberside Factory Trawlers (Filleters). Pict also was the last of the type built for British Owners. She was delivered in July 1983.

In 1974, her first full year of fishing, Pict caught 2672 tonnes (estimated) and was the 7th British trawler in the Dolphin Competition.

During bad weather off the Norwegian coast on the 9th February 1974, the day after Gaul is thought to have gone missing, Pict was dodging head to wind when at about 1500 she met a terrific sea head on, which stopped the ship altogether. Considerable damage was done to the plating on the front of the bridge.

During the fish bobbers' strike at Hull in December 1974 after a good trip to the Norwegian coast she docked at Blyth after only 35 days landing 200 tonnes of fillets.

One of the hazards of trawling is fouling another ship's trawl. This happened to Pict off the Norwegian coast when she fouled gear with a Norwegian Sidewinder. By agreement the Norwegian chopped off her warps to let the bigger Pict haul all the gear to sort it out. While it was coming

aboard, a wire parted and netting was taffled round the propeller resulting in Pict having to be towed into Vardo by another B.U.T. ship.

The previous Pict H162, built in 1936, was requisitioned for service in the Royal Navy during the Second World War. In 1982 during the Falklands conflict the modern Pict had the chance to serve her country as a minesweeper. Pict arrived in Hull on the 12th April 1982 from the Norwegian grounds and after landing 400 tonnes of frozen blocks sailed to join the 3 Marr trawlers at Rosyth arriving on 20th April. She returned to Hull from duty in the South Atlantic in November 1982. By October 1983 with no quotas for white fish Pict was re-equipped to go shrimp fishing at Spitzbergen. Her fillet lines were removed and she took on 10 Norwegian deckhands. By early 1985 the Pict was the last Humberside freezer still operating as a trawler, but on the 10th July 1985 she sailed as a guard ship to the English Channel. On the 8th August 1986 she was sold to International Fishing Investments, Channel Islands, and in 1987 began fishing at the Falklands with Skipper Peter Costello.

Still named Pict. Fishing from Falklands Reg. at Guernsey.

ROMAN

Rear Admiral Lucey was the Commander of the frigates on support duties off Iceland and his wife was asked to name the Roman as a tribute to the Royal Navy's assistance to British trawlers over the years. High winds prevented her being launched at the time of the naming ceremony and she entered the waters of the lower Clyde the following day. She was the last ship to be built for the B.U.T. fleet.

Name	Reg. No.	Off. No.	Tons	Length/ Breadth	Call Sign
Roman	GY 253	359903	1448	210.0	GUDY
			537	41.0	

Builder	Type
Ferguson Bros. (Pt Glas) Ltd Port Glasgow 1974	Wholefish Freezer

Factory Details

30,000 cu.ft. fish hold
6 x 20 Station Jackstone Froster V.P. freezers capable of freezing 37.5 tons per day in 42″ x 21″ x 4″ blocks

Engine Details

Mirrlees Blackstone Ltd.
Type K Major 6
3180 BHP 13½ knots

Launched	Skipper Maiden Voyage	Crew No.
11th December 1973	Peter Pulfrey	24

Named by

Mrs Barbara Lucey, wife of Rear Admiral M.N. Lucey, Flag Officer Scotland and N. Ireland

After running fishing trials off the West coast of Scotland Roman sailed round to her home port of Grimsby. She sailed on her maiden voyage on the 28th June 1974 for the Norwegian coast, commanded by Skipper Peter Pulfrey.

After only 4 years sailing from Grimsby, Roman and her crew were transferred to fish out of Hull in 1978, along with

Roman was towed home by St. Jerome which was homeward bound at the time and reached Hull on the 24th August 1978.

After repairs Roman returned to fishing. In 1985 B.U.T. sold her to a Greenland owner for fishing out of Godthab.

Now Roman I fishing from Greenland
X Roman 1985

THOMAS HAMLINGS

Thomas Hamlings was a partnership between, the smack owner Tommy Hamling and the Hull Lord Mayor, George Hall, who had many business interests and helped finance the venture. The partnership flourished and a company was formed in 1893. Tommy Hamling, whose ambition was to own the fastest horse-drawn vehicle in the area, was unfortunately killed in a traffic accident when his own horse-drawn vehicle over turned.

In the course of time Harold Hall became Chairman of the company followed by his son Harold Watson Hall who remained as Chairman until the company closed in 1983. Thomas Boyd who was Manager for 39 years left in 1936 to form his own fishing company.

In the mid 1930's with the discovery of rich fishing grounds in the Barents Sea, Thomas Hamlings started to build up its fleet with larger 170 feet trawlers to fish these grounds, the first being "Pentland Firth" built for the

all the other B.U.T. freezers. During 1978 Roman was having a successful year and was one of Britain's top ships. On the 12th August 1978 Roman commanded by Skipper Terry Baskcombe was fishing off Bear Island when at 10 a.m. a serious fire broke out in the engine room. 3 factory hands who went in to fight the fire were overcome by smoke and fumes and despite repeated attempts by officers wearing breathing apparatus to reach them they were lost. Roman was blacked out by the blaze, but Ross Vanguard with Skipper Peter Costello came to her aid and tried to put the fire hoses on board, but these parted because Roman had no steerage control. Roman's sister ship Goth with Skipper Jock Kerr came on the scene and after 10 survivors had been transferred to Ross Vanguard, Goth took the stricken trawler in tow to Honningsvaag. Roman had been at sea for 53 days when the tragedy struck and she had caught 350 tonnes of fish. The men lost were Ken Dean, Alan Parkin and Henry Sinkins.

subsidiary, Firth S.T. Co. These fine ships were requisitioned by the Navy for service during the 2nd World War.

As the rebuilding of the fleet began in 1945, a black band was placed in the funnel colours in remembrance of Donald Hall who fell whilst fighting in the rearguard at Dunkirk with the East Yorkshire Yeomanry, the whole regiment being either captured or killed.

From 1948 until 1962 new sidewinders were built at Beverley and then in 1964 the first of 5 freezer stern trawlers was built as the Company enjoyed the success of the 1950's, to the 1970's.

In the 1980's with no profitable grounds left to fish for Britain's deep-sea trawler fleet, most major fishing companies were fighting a losing battle to keep in business. Despite a major campaign for Government support for the industry by Thomas Hamlings Managing Director, Jonathan Watson Hall, no help was forthcoming and the Company had to close in 1983.

NAME THEME: Lesser known saints.
FUNNEL: Black top, buff with a wide orange band. A black band separates the orange and buff.
HULL: Black with yellow line.

Name	Reg. No.	Off. No.	Tons	Length/Breadth	Call Sign
St. Benedict	H 164	359161	1454	245.0	GRHM
			678	41.5	

Builder	Type
Ferguson Bros (P/GL) Ltd. Port Glasgow, 1973	Wholefish Freezer

Factory Details

34,000cu.ft. fish hold
9 x 20 Station Jackstone Froster V.P. freezers able to freeze 14,000lb (1,000 stone) every 3 hours or 54 tons per day.

Engine Details

British Polar Ltd.
2860 BHP 15½ knots

Launched	Skipper Maiden Voyage	Crew No.
30th August 1972	Trevor Doyle	28

Named by

Mrs S. Robinson, wife of Thomas Hamlings Manager

ST BENEDICT

The St. Benedict was built at a cost of £1.5 million and at the time of her entry into fishing, she carried some of the most sophisticated electronic fishing aids available. She was also the first Humberside trawler fitted with twin arenas, that allowed her to haul one trawl and shoot another straight away, so that mending could be done without the loss of fishing time.

St. Benedict sailed from Hull in February 1973 for her maiden voyage to the Norwegian coast, commanded by Skipper Trevor Doyle. Trawling began NSW of the Lofoten Islands and in her first 36 hours, 2 daylight and 1 night's fishing, she caught 56 tonnes of fish. St. Benedict returned to Hull after a trip of 54 days to land 600 tonnes of blocks.

In June 1974 St. Benedict, commanded by Skipper Alan Blenkin, on returning from her 7th trip set up a new British record, with a catch of 707.25 tonnes from a 56 day trip to the Barents Sea and Norwegian Coast. The catch was mostly cod and haddock, and 300 kits of mixed. During the trip fishing was spasmodic and the biggest single haul, whilst on pelagic trawl, was lost when both cod lines broke. The catch took $3\frac{1}{2}$ days to land. During the next 18 months she set up 2 more records, 775 tonnes (December 1974), 777 tonnes (June 1985).

Most successful trawler Skippers, if they were firm but fair, kept the same crew with them over the years, even transferring to other ships together. This was the case with St. Benedict and regular Skipper Trevor Doyle and his crew, all of whom served at least 5 years together.

As the opportunity to fish the traditional grounds ran out, the big freezers had to look to fishing in other areas: Cornwall, the Scilly Isles, Irish Coast, Rockall to the Faroe Islands. In April 1974 St. Benedict was chartered by the W.F.A. to explore for Blue Whiting grounds, her catch of 66 tonnes being used for tests.

In 1979 between April and May, St. Benedict did 3 trips catching blue whiting for Findus Frozen Foods, catching between 750-820 tonnes per trip for an average 18 days. The bigger fish were for human consumption and the smaller ones for pet food. On a 36 day trip to Rockall 758 tonnes of prime haddock was caught. The rest of the time was spent on Mackerel fishing mainly for the Dutch market.

In 1983 with the closure of Hamlings, St. Benedict was laid up in Albert Dock to await a new owner. In 1984 she was sold to Panamanian Interests at the knockdown price

Photo by courtesy of Walter Fussey & Son.

of £500,000, a reflection on the state of the fishing industry. She was placed under the Moroccan flag but due to her owner being unable to obtain fishing licences her white hull became a landmark in Hull's Albert Dock. A sad waste of such a fine ship. In 1986 she was sold to Sea Lords Products of Nelson, New Zealand, and after a refit she left Hull to fish from New Zealand.

Now Will Watch fishing New Zealand.
X Al Mustafa 1986
X St. Benedict 1984

ST. FINBARR

St. Finbarr sailed on her maiden voyage direct from the shipbuilder's yard on the 26th November 1964. Skipper Sawyer took her to Greenland, Labrador and Newfoundland. She arrived at her home port of Hull on the 25th January 1965, landing 440 tonnes of fish.

From her second voyage she set up a new national record

Name	Reg. No.	Off. No.	Tons	Length/ Breadth	Call Sign
St. Finbarr	H 308	305772	1139	210.6	GPXV
			505	36.4	

Builder	Type
Ferguson Bros Ltd. Port Glasgow 1964	Wholefish Freezer

Factory Details

25,750 cu.ft.
4 x 12 Jackstone Froster plate freezers
30 tons per day in 100lb blocks

Engine Details

Mirrlees National Ltd.
Type KLSS M8
1592 BHP 13½ knots

Launched	Skipper Maiden Voyage	Crew No.
26th September 1964	Tom Sawyer	25

Named by

Miss Alanna Watson Hall, daughter of Mr. Harold
Watson Hall, Chairman of owners.

catch of 488 tonnes 17 cwt. mainly of cod from a 37 day trip
to Labrador. On her best fishing day she had 2 good hauls
of 900 and 500 baskets. For these she towed only 20
minutes.

St. Finbarr proved to be so successful her owners ordered
3 more similar design freezer stern trawlers from Ferguson
Bros. these being St. Jason, St. Jasper and St. Jerome.

St. Finbarr sailed from Hull on the 16th November 1966,
on her 14th voyage. On Christmas eve she was positioned
about 100 miles off the coast of Labrador. Due to bad
weather trawling was postponed and the off-duty crew
allowed to rest for Christmas day.

About 0730 a fire broke out in the accommodation area
which spread very rapidly and gave the crew little chance of
firefighting. Skipper Sawyers sent out a Mayday which was
answered immediately by "Orsino", only 5 miles away.
Suddenly a blast of hot air blew out the wheelhouse door
and bridge windows and hurled Skipper Sawyers out of the
bridge onto the engine room casing. The fire then spread to
the bridge and the Skipper gave orders to prepare to
abandon ship.

Photo by courtesy of Appledore Ferguson Shipbuilders Ltd.

The Orsino in freezing conditions (14°F) picked up the exhausted survivors (sadly 12 men were lost) except for the Skipper, mate and Ch. Engineer who remained on board the St. Finbarr.

Later men from "Orsino" crossed to St. Finbarr with warm clothes for the 3 men remaining on her, but by 1400 she was burning so fiercely Skipper Sawyers decided to abandon her. At 1600 a boarding party established a tow and Orsino commanded by Skipper Eddie Wooldridge set out to tow St. Finbarr stern first to St. Johns, Newfoundland, 600 miles to the south. But as the tow was undertaken in bad weather driving snow and gale force winds, Skipper Wooldridge headed for St. Anthony's, a small harbour only 250 miles away.

On the 26th at 0800 the tow parted but towing was resumed at 1800 the same day. Next day the 27th the St. Finbarr gradually began to settle by the head, and at 1925 she finally sank, just 40 miles from land, having been towed over 200 miles.

13 crewmen survived the tragedy from the crew of 25. It is worth noting 40 ships of various nationalities responded to come to the aid of St. Finbarr.

The men lost were John Smith, James Hamilton, Harry Smith, Stanley Brigham, Johan Sigurdsson, John Matthews, Robert Coulman, Kenneth Pullen, J. O'Dell, Arthur Harrison, Thomas Gray, David Young.

ST. JASON

Name	Reg. No.	Off. No.	Tons	Length/ Breadth	Call Sign
St. Jason	H 436	334062	1288 451	231.1 39.4	GYCB

Builder	Type
Ferguson Bros. (P.GL) Ltd.	Wholefish Freezer

Factory Details

32,000 cu.ft. fish hold
8 x 20 Station Jackstone Froster V.P. freezers
On 2 levels 4 top flat 4 lower flat.
Capable of freezing 700 kits heads on 850, kits headless per day.
Baader 163 header.

Engine Details

British Polar Engines Ltd.
Type M66T
2160 BHP 14 knots

Launched	Skipper Maiden Voyage	Crew No.
9th August 1967	Tom Sawyer	28-31

Named by

Mrs Clarissa Watson Hall, wife of Mr. Jonathan Watson Hall, Director of T. Hamlings

The St. Jason was the first of a class of 3 sister trawlers from the Ferguson Bros. Yard. She ran her fishing trials in

The "Northella". Photo by courtesy of Ian Andrews.

The "Orsino". Photo by courtesy of Peter Horsley.

Scottish waters in December 1967. The command of St. Jason was given to Skipper Tom Sawyer, who along with St. Finbarr had proved to be so successful in Thomas Hamlings' entry into freezer stern trawling in 1964.

On the 20th December 1967 St. Jason sailed from the builder's yard direct to the Newfoundland and Labrador fishing grounds and after a trip of 54 days she arrived at her home port of Hull for the first time on the 12th February 1968, to land 502 tonnes of mainly cod. During the trip the winch broke down due to dirt in the hydraulics. The Norwegian winch makers flew a mechanic to St. Johns, Newfoundland and he worked non-stop for 36 hours to repair the winch and allow St. Jason to resume fishing.

For her second trip Skipper Sawyer took St. Jason to the White Sea and Bear Island and from a 45 day trip landed a good catch of 648.5 tonnes which was just 17 tonnes short of the British record of that time.

St. Jason through her career was always one of Britain's top trawlers. Her best position in the Dolphin Bowl was 4th, but she was never lower than 15th.

Photo by courtesy of Appledore Ferguson Shipbuilders Ltd.

From the mid 1970's St. Jason, like other British freezers, began to fish herring, mackerel, skad, and blue whiting in home waters. The catches of whitefish were still landed at Hull, but herring and mackerel were landed in Holland which had better landing facilities for this type of fish; a 660 ton catch could be discharged in 12 hours. The fish after being processed was usually sold to 3rd world countries to help feed their people. In December 1982 St. Jason, with Skipper Arthur Ball, landed her catch at Ijmuiden. Her crew then came home to Hull for Christmas leave but they were destined never to return due to Thomas Hamlings having to close down. After spending years laid idle, St. Jason was sold to Dutch owners on the 24th November 1986. In 1987 St. Jason was acquired by Seaboard Offshore Aberdeen for fishing at the Falkland Isles.

Now Mount Kent still fishing reg. Aberdeen
X St. Jason 1987

ST. JASPER

The St. Jasper ran her fishing trials on the 30th January 1969 and then sailed round to Hull from the Clyde, during which she encountered a force 9 gale. Due to being a light ship (not all stores, fuel and water loaded) she gave her non-seagoing guests a rough ride, some of whom would take much persuading to visit the ship again. She arrived at her home port, Hull, on the 2nd February 1969, to become the port's 21st freezer stern trawler.

St. Jasper sailed from Hull on her maiden voyage on the 9th February 1969, commanded by Skipper Ernest Johnson. The trawler did not encounter any major problems and

Name	Reg. No.	Off. No.	Tons	Length/ Breadth	Call Sign
St. Jasper	H 31	334107	1286	231.1	GYZW
			451	39.4	

Builder	Type
Ferguson Bros (P/GL) Ltd.	Wholefish
Port Glasgow 1968	Freezer

Factory Details

32,000 cu.ft. fish hold
8 x 20 Station Jackstone Froster V.P. freezers.
On 2 levels 4 top flat 4 lower flat.
Capable of freezing 700 kits heads on 850 kits headless per day.
Baader 163 header.

Engine Details

British Polar Engines Ltd.
Type M66T
2160 BHP 14 knots

Launched	Skipper Maiden Voyage	Crew No.
14th August 1968	Ernest Johnson	28

Named by

Mrs G.E. Wilson, wife of the Secretary of T. Hamlings

Photo by courtesy of Appledore Ferguson Shipbuilders Ltd.

The ship's engine room crew were responsible for the factory deck machinery and winches as well as the engine room. The chief engineer was on call at all times and the 2nd engineer and a greaser split the watches with the 3rd engineer and a greaser, working 6 hours on, 6 hours off.

St. Jasper and her sisters were a highly successful class of trawlers and they always ranked high in the Dolphin Bowl competition.

In 1975 Skipper Johnson started to take St. Jasper mackerel fishing from October until March fishing at the Minches and Cornwall, and averaging 500 tonnes for 21 days.

In the late 1970's Thomas Hamlings for two seasons

during her 56 day trip to the White Sea and Bear Island grounds good supplies of fish were found and a very good catch of 650 tonnes of blocks was landed at Hull. Her Chief Engineer was Hugh Williams and her mate was Arthur Ball.

(Above) The "Princess Anne". Photo by courtesy of Walter Fussey & Son.

The "Arctic Ranger" – symbol of hope for the future. Photo by courtesy of Walter Fussey & Son.

during the winter sent St. Jasper and her sisters into the Baltic to Klondike Baltic cod (which had a good flavour), first from Polish trawlers and then the next year from German trawlers. This was yet another attempt by a British owner to find work for his ships.

In 1983 with the closure of her owners St. Jasper was laid up in Albert Dock, Hull, until her sale to Seaboard Offshore of Inverness on the 1st October 1984. She was converted into a standby safety vessel.

Now Seaboard Integrity standby vessel.
X St. Jasper 1985

ST. JEROME

After running her trials in Scottish waters, the St. Jerome arrived at her home port of Hull for the first time on the 23rd April 1968. She was to become one of Britain's top trawlers and held the record for the most fish caught in a trip by a British freezer trawler for the incredibly long time of 5 years 7 months.

The St. Jerome sailed from Hull on her maiden voyage in early May 1968, commanded by Skipper Mervyn Hough, who took her fishing at Newfoundland and Labrador. For her trip of nearly 2 months she landed 580 tonnes.

The St. Jerome set up her first British record when she arrived at Hull on the 27th November 1968 and landed 680 tonnes of mainly cod from a 63 day trip to Spitzbergen and the White Sea. Her Skipper, Mervyn Hough, had been flown home after 2 weeks due to falling ill, and Skipper J. Nelson had completed the trip. In May 1969, St. Jerome

Name	Reg. No.	Off. No.	Tons	Length/ Breadth	Call Sign
St. Jerome	H 442	334078	1288	231.1	GYNR
			451	39.4	

Builder	Type
Ferguson Bros. (P.GL) Ltd. Port Glasgow 1968	Wholefish Freezer

Factory Details

32,000 cu.ft. fish hold
8 x 20 Station Jackstone Froster V.P. freezers.
On 2 levels 4 top flat 4 lower flat.
Capable of freezing 700 kits heads on, 850 kits headless per day.
Baader 163 header.

Engine Details

British Polar Engines Ltd.
Type M66T 5 cyl
2160 BHP 14½ knots

Launched	Skipper Maiden Voyage	Crew No.
7th November 1967	Mervyn Hough	26

Named by

Miss Jennifer Watson Hall, daughter of Mr. Harold Watson Hall, Chairman of owners.

broke her own record when on the 16th May she arrived in Hull to land 691 tonnes of frozen wholefish, from a trip of only 31 days to the White Sea with Skipper M. Hough. This trip is thought to be the best ever by a Hull trawler. The record stood until June 1974 when it was beaten by Hamlings St. Benedict. During 1969 St. Jerome caught a total of 3820 tonnes of fish.

In 1979 St. Jerome went to fish herring off the coast of Scotland. Her owners were under the impression they had government permission to fish there. But soon a British Fishery Protection Vessel ordered her to stop fishing. During the next three weeks Hamlings awaited the Ministry of Fishing to grant permission to resume fishing. All this time the St. Jerome lay idle, her crew having to suffer the taunts of the Dutch trawlers fishing the grounds around her. Permission to fish came two days before the end of the season, causing the trip to be a financial disaster for Hamlings and the crew.

Whilst fishing at Labrador in Arctic weather conditions, a few miles off the ice edge, St. Jerome fouled her propeller with her trawl. Although this was a common occurence, among ice it was difficult to get free. But fortunately her sister trawler, commanded by Skipper Arthur Ball, was fishing close by and took her in tow. Due to the amount of ice, St. Johns, Newfoundland, was closed to shipping and it took nine days to reach the ice free port of St. Pierre in the south of Newfoundland.

In 1983 with no profitable fishing areas left for their fleet, Hamlings closed and St. Jerome was put up for sale. After spending many months laid up alongside her sister St. Jasper in Hull's Albert Dock, on the 29th October 1984 St. Jerome was sold to Seaboard Offshore and registered at Inverness. She was converted into a standby safety vessel.

Now Seaboard Intrepid standby vessel.
X St. Jerome 1985

Photo by courtesy of Appledore Ferguson Shipbuilders Ltd.

HELLYER BROTHERS LTD.

During the middle of the nineteenth century, Charles and Robert Hellyer brought their Smack to Hull from Brixham. In 1888 they founded Hellyer Steam Fishing Co. Ltd. fishing the North Sea with a steam trawler fleet. In 1913 they pioneered the use of the wireless in their ships. The Company became Hellyer Bros. Ltd., in 1919.

During the 1930's a fleet of big deep-water trawlers was built which were named after ancient tribes. The Company also ran a joint company, Northern Fishing Co. Ltd.

After the 1939-45 War the Company, also known as the Devon Fishing Co., received back several trawlers from Naval Service and under cousins, Graham Hellyer and

Mark Hellyer, who became joint managers, the Company was built up. One of its major expansions was in 1960 when Hellyer's became the controlling interest in the large Hull firm, Kingston S.F. Co. Ltd. Then in 1963 they amalgamated with Associated Fisheries and took over the remnants of the Lord Line Fleet, which included the stern trawler Lord Nelson. In 1966 4 freezer stern trawlers were built for the fleet.

In 1969 Hellyer Bros became one of the major constituents of British United Trawlers. Graham Hellyer becoming Managing Director of B.U.T., Mark Hellyer joining the Board.

NAME THEME: Ancient tribes and Shakespearian Characters
FUNNEL: Yellow with blue flag containing a white 'H'
HULL: Grey

CASSIO

Cassio the second ship of her class arrived in Hull from the Scottish building yard on the 27th September 1966.

For her maiden voyage Skipper J.C. Lilley took Cassio to fish the Newfoundland and Labrador grounds. Although it was early in the season and the ship had the usual teething problems she returned to Hull after 56 days with a good catch of 400 tonnes of codling.

In August 1968 the Cassio, commanded by Skipper Jack Lilley, had the distinction of being chosen to represent Britain at the International Fisheries Exhibition at Leningrad, USSR. After spending 10 days in Hull fish dock being

Name	Reg. No.	Off. No.	Tons	Length/Breadth	Call Sign
Cassio	H 398	308558	1574	223.9	GSGU
			672	39.1	

Builder	Type
Yarrow & Co. Ltd. Glasgow 1966	Wholefish Freezer

Factory Details
27,000 cu.ft. 2 holds
10 L. Sterne V.P. Freezers
4 over No2 Hold
6 over No1 Hold
Capable of freezing 30 tons per day

Engine Details
Mirrlees National Ltd.
Type KLSSMR 8
2350 BHP 13½ knots

Launched	Skipper Maiden Voyage	Crew No.
5th April 1966	Jack Lilley	25

Named by
Mrs Pamela Joy Milne, wife of Mr. M. Milne, a Director of Asst. Fisheries.

painted and cleaned, she sailed from Hull to Leningrad on the 31st July 1968. Her crew of 17 were specially kitted out for the occasion. After 4 days at sea she arrived at Leningrad 3 days before the opening of the Exhibition. Over the next 14 days she was visited by approximately 35,000 visitors. 09.00 - 13.00 was for the technical parties and 13.00 to

Photo by courtesy of Walter Fussey & Son.

20.00 for the public. Cassio was held in high esteem by the Russians because she had been built on the Clyde, where so many famous ships had been built in the past.

After the Exhibition in 1968 Cassio was the first British trawler to experiment with a pelagic trawl.

On the 1st January 1972 while fishing off North West Iceland, at about 7 a.m. a fire broke out in the accommodation and although considerable damage was done the crew managed to put the fire out. Fortunately no-one was injured. Skipper Lilley took Cassio in to Isafjord, while Miranda and Odin stood by her. She was able to return to Hull under her own power and arrived back in Hull on the night of the 5th January 1972. She had sailed from Hull on the 2nd December 1972. She landed 200 tonnes of fish.

On the 30th July 1978 Cassio sailed from Hull to join her 2 sisters to fish out of Port Albany, Australia, commanded by Skipper Neville Beavers, with a crew of 22.

Now Orsirichainava 6 fishing from Bangkok for Thailand owners.

X Honey 1 1986
X Cassio 1984

CORIOLANUS

Name	Reg. No.	Off. No.	Tons	Length/ Breadth	Call Sign
Coriolanus	H 412	308578	1105	223.9	GSJH
			360	39.1	

Builder	Type
Yarrow & Co. Ltd. Glasgow 1967	Factory Freezer

Factory Details	Baader Equipment
375 tons 27,000 cu.ft. fish hold 2 x 11 Station Jackstone Froster H.P. Freezers able to freeze 24 tons of fillets per day	Type 99 gutter 2 type 188 filleters able to cope with 37 tons per day

Engine Details
Mirrlees National Ltd. Type KLSSMR 8 2350 BHP 15½ knots

Launched	Skipper Maiden Voyage	Crew No.
30th November 1966	Maurice Ward	38

Named by
Mrs M. Noble wife of a director of Associated Fisheries.

Coriolanus was launched at the Clydeholm Yard of Barclay Curl Co. and completed by Yarrow. She was the fourth sister ship in her class and the last of the 7 stern trawlers built for Associated/Hellyer. She was also the only fillet factory trawler in the fleet. Her builders, "Yarrow", were renowned for the warships they had built for the Royal Navy over the years, mainly destroyers and frigates. Coriolanus cost £700,000 to build.

Coriolanus, Humberside's first factory freezer, arrived at her home port of Hull on the 13th May 1967, and sailed on her maiden voyage on the 28th May. Skipper M. Ward took her fishing first at Greenland and then to Newfoundland. Her role was to produce 28lb blocks of fish block for Birds Eye fish sticks. For this process each fish had to be boned, filleted and skinned. Only 28% of the whole fish was usable. For a 9 week trip a catch of 290 tonnes was landed but she had caught over 1,000 tonnes of fish. The offal was turned into fish meal by a plant on board.

Coriolanus is reputed to have led a reasonably quiet life, never involved in tragedies or strandings, except on three occasions during December 1977. On 1st December whilst in the Lockpits, outward bound for Spitzbergen, due to a fire in the galley, she had to return to her berth. On 6th December a few hours after leaving Hull three small fires, one in galley, two in accommodation, meant her having to return to Hull. On 9th December, she sailed again, but had to return to Hull because of crew trouble. Police were called on board when she docked and a crew member was taken into custody.

In 1969 Coriolanus became part of the B.U.T. fleet until the 30th May 1980 when she was sold to Greek interests.

Now Achaios fishing from Piraeus, Greece
X Coriolanus 1980

ORSINO

Orsino arrived at Hull from the Clyde on the 8th December 1966. She sailed from Hull on the 14th December 1966 for her maiden voyage. She was commanded by the well-respected Skipper Edward Wooldridge, affectionately known as "Alamein Eddie" from his war service. It was his first voyage in command of a stern trawler and it proved to be a very dramatic one, by being involved in the St. Finbarr tragedy. She arrived back in Hull on the 16th February 1967, having been delayed 12 days in Canada. She landed 8,322 blocks of fish weighing 480 tonnes.

Name	Reg. No.	Off. No.	Tons	Length/ Breadth	Call Sign
Orsino	H 410	308566	1574	223.9	GSJA
			672	39.1	

Builder	Type
Yarrow & Co. Ltd. Glasgow 1966	Wholefish Freezer

Factory Details

27,000 cu.ft.
10 L. Stern V.P. Freezers
6 Over No 1 hold
4 Over No 2 hold
Able to freeze 30 tons per day

Engine Details

Mirrlees National Ltd.
Type KLSSMR 8
2350 BHP 13½ knots

Launched	Skipper Maiden Voyage	Crew No.
30th August 1966	Edward A. Wooldridge	25

Named by

Mrs Lydia Barrowman, wife of a Director of Associated Fisheries

Britain's First Mother Ship

During severe winter weather conditions in 1968, Hull lost three trawlers with 58 men in the space of three weeks. The public outcry at this disaster was channelled by a group of trawlermen's wives to pressurise the Government into acquiring the services of a British mother ship, to assist the fleet at Iceland in the winter months. Orsino was chartered by the Board of Trade, and after modifications for weather and medical duties she sailed from Hull on the 29th November 1968. She spent the next 154 days at sea commanded by Skipper Wooldridge, who was relieved for 35 days by Skipper Laurie Oliver.

Orsino was also chartered for the winter of 1969-70. She was again commanded by Skipper Wooldridge. She sailed from Hull on the 26th November 1969, with 28 crew including a weather advisor, meteorologist and a doctor. She returned to Hull on the 29th March 1970 finishing her mother ship duties.

On the 23rd April 1975 while Orsino was bunkering at

Honningsvaag a fire broke out in the accommodation. Sadly the 2nd mate, David Thompson, was overcome by fumes whilst fighting the fire and was lost. She was beached away from the port and later towed back to Hull by the Kurd, arriving in Hull on the 9th May 1975.

Some Log Details

Days at Sea: 154
Steamed: 6,210 miles
Gale & Ice Warnings: 189 issued
Signals Sent: 3,104
Signals Received: 5,580
Lowest Recorded Temp: -17°C

Trawlers Fishing Her Area

Average: 18 per day
Highest No: 81 in a day
Trawler Trips Made: 243

Orsino left Hull for Port Albany, Australia on the 14th January 1978 with a mixed crew of Hull and Grimsby men, commanded by Grimsby Skipper Peter Crane. She was to fish for the Southern Ocean Fish Processing Pty Ltd., a company in which B.U.T. had a 50% holding.

Now Jessie 1 Panamanian Reg.
X Orsino 1984

OTHELLO

Name	Reg. No.	Off. No.	Tons	Length/Breadth	Call Sign
Othello	H 389	308550	1574	223.9	GRZA
			672	39.1	

Builder	Type
Yarrow & Co. Ltd. Glasgow 1966	Wholefish Freezer

Factory Details

27,000 cu.ft.
10 L. Stern V.P. Freezers
6 Over No 1 hold
4 Over No 2 hold
Able to freeze 30 tons per day

Engine Details

Mirrlees National Ltd.
Type KLSSMR 8
2350 BHP 13½ knots

Launched	Skipper Maiden Voyage	Crew No.
9th December 1965	Maurice Ward	25

Named by

Mrs J. Bennett, wife of the Managing Director of Associated Fisheries Ltd.

The Othello was the first British freezer stern trawler with an engine room aft. Her factory deck could be converted to filleting if necessary. She arrived at Hull on the 20th June 1966.

For her maiden voyage Skipper Ward took Othello to Greenland and then to the Newfoundland grounds. From a 7 week trip she landed 400 tonnes of headless codstuffs. Skipper Jack Lilley was passenger Skipper, due to him taking the Cassio.

On the 6th January 1969 Othello commanded by Skipper Neville Beavers was fishing about 120 miles off Svino, Norway, when a fire broke out in the accommodation. At 5.55 a Mayday was sent out which was answered by Ross Aquila in a position 8 miles away. Although the crew tried to fight the fire it spread very rapidly. However they managed to batten down the engine room, to save it from damage. The 25 crew were forced to abandon ship in 4 life-rafts. They were picked up by Ross Aquila commanded by Skipper Henry Sloan. Early next day Ross Aquila'a mate, Tom Atkins, rowed Skipper Beavers back to the red hot Othello and the Skipper went on board, and a tow line was attached. At 9.30am Ross Aquila in bad weather began

the tow to Trondheim, which was reached on the 8th January. Later Othello was towed home to Hull arriving on the 20th January. In April she went for repair on the River Wear, at a cost of £350,000, half of the cost of building her. During the tow the Ross Aquila's cook had to work hard to feed 45 men in bad weather, a feat he was highly praised for.

In May 1972 Othello, with Skipper Frank Drewery, and Kingston Amber, with Skipper Malcolm Clark, picked up the crew of the Faroese trawler Sonderberg, which sank in a severe storm 370 miles east north east of St. Johns, Newfoundland. After picking up the distress signals the Hull ships arrived to rescue the crew from their life-rafts, an hour after they had abandoned Sonderberg. Othello took 36 crew on board and Kingston Amber picked up her Skipper and mate, who when the weather moderated were transferred to Othello.

All the crew were saved. The Faroese Government later made awards to the British crews, to thank them for their part in the rescue. In the winter of 1972-73 Othello served as a support ship for the British fleet. On the 24th September 1977, Othello, commanded by Skipper Dick Spence, left Hull for Port Albany, Australia to fish for Southern Ocean Fish Processors Pty Ltd. She was laid up for several years.

Now Tasanee, Panamanian reg.
X Othello 1984

| Associated Fisheries | Boston Deep Sea Fisheries | Boyd Line | British United Trawlers | Thomas Hamlings | Hellyer Bros |

| Hudson Bros | Lord Line | J. Marr & Son | Newington Trawlers | Ranger Fishing Company | Ross Group |

J. MARR & SON LTD.

J. Marr & Son, are descendants of Joseph Marr, the Hull merchant and smack owner of the 1870's. In 1902 the firm's head office was moved to Fleetwood, but in the late 1920's the Trident S.F.Co. and the City S.F.Co. were acquired to build up a fleet at Hull. In 1934 Westella, the first of the Company's "Ella" trawlers was built, followed by Kirkella in 1936. Westella was lost while in Naval service at the Dunkirk withdrawal in June 1940.

After World War 2 the Company's rebuilding programme began under Chairman Geoffrey Edwards Marr and his brother Leslie James Marr. The Company went on to become one of Britain's major family fishing concerns. Mr.G.E. Marr's son, Alan, joined the firm in 1951 and Mr. L.J. Marr's son, Andrew, in 1959. In 1958 pioneering work began on freezing fish at sea on 2 of J. Marr's sidewinders, which in 1962 resulted in the first of 10 wholefish freezer stern trawlers being built for the Hull fleet. Mr. G. Alan Marr succeeded his father as Chairman in 1969.

With the decline of the fishing industry in the 1980's J. Marr & Son moved into the scientific research field of shipping. Mr Andrew Marr became Chairman of Andrew Marr International Ltd., which operates the freezer trawlers, Westella and Kirkella.

Mr. G. Alan Marr's son, Charles, now manages the Company's highly successful fresher stern-trawler fleet based at Hull, and in 1988 took delivery of 2 new fresher stern trawlers the Lancella and Thornella, built at Selby.

NAMES: Ending with "Ella"
FUNNEL: Red with black top
HULL: Yellow with red line

CORDELLA

Name	Reg. No.	Off. No.	Tons	Length/ Breadth	Call Sign
Cordella	H 177	359181	1450 427	230.3 41.7	GTAB

Builder	Type
Clelands Shipbuilding Co.Ltd. Wallsend 1973	Wholefish Freezer

Factory Details

35,000 cu.ft. fish hold
10 x 20 Jackstone Froster V.P. Freezers capable of freezing 46 tons per day in 100lb blocks.
Type 28 Stetland Gutter

Engine Details

Mirrlees Blackstone
Type KMR Major 7
3246 BHP 16½ knots

Launched	Skipper Maiden Voyage	Crew No.
6th February 1973	Ronald Boughen	24

Named by

Mrs R.J. Gledhill, wife of Superintendent Engineer of J. Marr

Shipwrights preparing for the launch of the "Junella" in 1975. Photo copyright of Swan Hunter Shipbuilders Ltd.

The naming of the "Junella" in 1975. Left to right: Mr. Boyd, Shipyard Manager, Mrs. Diane Drever, Miss Alison Drever, Skipper Charles Drever MBE. Photo copyright of Swan Hunter Shipbuilders Ltd.

(Above) The "Pict". Photo by courtesy of
Walter Fussey & Son.

The "C.S. Forester". Photo by courtesy of
Walter Fussey & Son.

High winds prevented Cordella being launched at the time of the naming ceremony and it was the next day she entered the waters of the Tyne. Cordella was the third of her class and was handed over on the 26th May 1973. She sailed a few days later direct to the Newfoundland fishing grounds, commanded by Skipper Ron Boughen.

Cordella's best fishing years: 1974, 6th Top British Trawler, 2705 tonnes; and 1975, 4th Top British Trawler, 1608 tonnes. From then she became a victim of tight quotas.

From 1980 Cordella was commanded by Skipper Dick Taylor and was involved in fishing for whitefish, mackerel, and herring, as both seasons and quotas allowed until the Falklands War in 1982, when after landing a catch of mackerel at Ings Haven, Holland, on the 11th April 1982 she was called up for service in the Royal Navy. On arriving at Rosyth, Cordella was chosen to become the flagship of the 5 Hull trawlers being converted into minesweepers for

service in the South Atlantic. Skipper Taylor stayed a week to advise the Senior Naval Officer on handling Cordella. While the 5 trawlers were in Naval Service the M.O.D. paid wages to all the crews of these ships who were unemployed. On the 5th November 1982 Cordella was returned to her owners and went to Immingham to be converted back to her fishing role.

In 1984 Cordella was chartered as a guard ship by Trinity House to work in the English Channel. Then later in the year she was chartered by Skeggs Seafoods of Nelson, New Zealand, leaving Hull in the early hours of the 1st December 1984 to begin her new career fishing in the southern oceans, with Skipper Anthony Barksworth and a crew which had been flown out from New Zealand.

Cordella still fishing in New Zealand.

FARNELLA

Farnella was the first of 3 sister trawlers built by Swan Hunter Small Ships Division. Delivered on the 24th April 1972, Farnella sailed direct from the Tyne to the North East Atlantic fishing grounds on the 27th April, commanded by Skipper Alfred Eagles. After a 59 day trip Farnella arrived in Hull for the first time on the 26th July 1972 and landed just under 400 tonnes of frozen blocks at a time when fishing stocks were low.

Farnella went on to become one of Britain's top trawlers. She was runner up to the Dane in the 1973 Dolphin Bowl Competition with 2684 tonnes, and she was never out of the top 20 chart of top British freezers.

Name	Reg. No.	Off. No.	Tons	Length/ Breadth	Call Sign
Farnella	H 135	342737	1469	230.3	GPHH
			518	41.8	

Builder	Type
Clelands Shipbuilding Co.Ltd.	Wholefish
Wallsend 1972	Freezer

Factory Details

35,000 cu.ft. fish hold
8 x 20 Station Jackstone Froster V.P. Freezers capable of freezing 600 kits in 24 hours in 100lb blocks.
800 cu.ft. Halibut room
Type 28 Shetland Gutter

Engine Details

Mirrlees Blackstone
Type KMP Major 6
2782 BHP 16½ knots

Launched	Skipper Maiden Voyage	Crew No.
2nd December 1971	Alfred Eagles	24

Named by

Mrs Else Marr, wife of Mr Andrew L. Marr, Director of J. Marr & Son

Farnella was one of five Hull freezers to serve in the Royal Navy as minesweepers during the Falklands War, being called upon to go to Rosyth on the 11th April 1982. She was returned to her owners on the 22nd October 1982 to convert back to fishing.

In 1984 Farnella's survey crew completed a highly suc-

cessful geographical survey of the seabed of the west coast of America for the United States Geographical Survey Department. Then in April 1986 after 5 years working in both trawling and survey work Farnella was given a £1.5 million conversion into a survey vessel, allowing her to take up a 5 year charter for the U.S. Geographical Survey Department.

Farnella now hydrographic geophysical survey vessel.

JUNELLA (1)

The Junella was the first British wholefish freezer trawler. She was the result of 4 years of research into freezing fish at sea, experiments having been carried out on the J. Marr sidewinders, Marbella and Junella.

Name	Reg. No.	Off. No.	Tons	Length/ Breadth	Call Sign
Junella (1)	H 347	301685	1435	240.7	GJQE
			588	38.7	

Builder	Type
Hall Russell & Co.Ltd. Aberdeen 1962	Wholefish Freezer

Factory Details

26,000 cu.ft.
11 x 12 Station L. Sterne V.P. freezers capable of freezing 25 tons of fish per day.
70lb blocks
Also special halibut blast freezer room

Engine Details

English Electric Co.
Diesel Electric
Type CSKPRM
3237 BHP 16 knots

Launched	Skipper Maiden Voyage	Crew No.
6th March 1962	Charles Drever Ch.Eng. Don Jarrett	24

Named by

Lady Chick, wife of Sir Louis Chick, Chairman of the White Fish Authority

She arrived at her home port of Hull from the builder's yard on the 11th July 1962, commanded by the 1961 Silver Cod winner, Skipper Charles Drever. By coincidence the Lord Nelson had returned from the fishing grounds on the same tide. Crowds of people on the riverside were able to see them both together.

Junella sailed from Hull on her maiden voyage on the 17th July 1962 for the Newfoundland grounds. She returned on the 19th August after 32 days and landed a capacity 5,500 kits of frozen fish, mainly cod.

On one of her early voyages Junella with Skipper Drever set up a national record of 420 tonnes of fish for a 42 day trip to Newfoundland.

In December 1965 whilst fishing at Iceland, Junella with Skipper C. Townend, along with other ships, stood by the 252 foot long West German stern trawler "Burgermeister Smidt" which had sprung a leak and was listing. Whilst being towed in huge waves and driving snow, the tow parted and she ran into an iceberg off Cape Farewell. Eventually her crew of 44 were taken off by nearby vessels. She was taken in tow by the "Weser" and the other ships poured oil on the water to break up the wave action but the

"Burgermeister Smidt" sank. Junella after having to go into Canada to replace the oil used, arrived back in Hull after a 47 days trip and landed 400 tonnes.

In June 1973 Junella was sold to the Atlantic Trawling Pty, a subsidiary of Amalgamated Fisheries of Hoot Bay, South Africa, and after being altered to fish for hake, she left to fish the southern oceans, renamed Bluefin Reg. CTA 124, on the 1st September 1973.

Now Southern Ranger registered in the Cayman Islands
X Bluefin 77
X Junella 73

Name details

This Junella was the 3rd J. Marr trawler to receive the name. The others were H 497 built at Selby 1948, sold to Grimsby by 1949, renamed Kirknes. H 399 built at Beverley 1947 as St. Crispin, became Junella 1951 to 1961. Renamed Farnella.

JUNELLA (2)

The other Junella had the distinction of being the first British wholefish freezer stern trawler, while this one to date has been the last built, having gone into service when the industry was going into decline.

For her maiden voyage Skipper A. Eagles took Junella to the Norwegian and White Sea fishing grounds and for a 60 day trip, landed 620 tonnes. The catch had to be carefully balanced because of quota restrictions, one third cod, one third haddock and the rest mixed White Sea species. For the success of the trip Skipper Eagles shared the credit with the

Name	Reg. No.	Off. No.	Tons	Length/ Breadth	Call Sign
Junella (2)	H 249	365586	1614 601	198.8 43.1	GUXU

Builder	Type
Clelands S.B. Co.Ltd. Wallsend 1975	Wholefish Freezer

Factory Details

30,000 cu.ft.
8 x 20 Station Jackstone Froster V.P. Freezers
160 block every 4 hours
Baader 166 gutting machine
42 tons per day

Engine Details

Mirrlees Blackstone Ltd.
Type KMR Major MKZ
3180 BHP 15 knots

Launched	Skipper Maiden Voyage	Crew No.
9th September 1975	Alfred Eagles	24-29

Named by

Mrs Diane Drever, wife of Skipper Charles Drever, M.B.E.

highly skilled veteran Chief Engineer, Don Jarrett, who had nursed the ship through minor breakdowns of equipment. Don Jarrett took nine Marr freezers on their maiden voyages, which was a fine achievement. In July 1978 whilst visiting Hull and Grimsby fish docks, Prince Charles expressed an interest in making a voyage on a trawler, and on April 21-23 1980 the Junella played host to Prince Charles whilst fishing off the Hebridean coast.

On the 28th September 1980 Junella was cast aground on rocks off the N.W. of Eilean Troday near the Isle of Skye, during a fierce night-time storm. Her crew of 29 men was taken off in a daring rescue by the Stornaway lifeboat, which had battled through heavy seas for 35 miles to reach the stricken trawler. The lifeboat had to go alongside 3 times to pick up the crew, Junella's Skipper being the last to leave. On the 1st October 1980 at 1 a.m. in atrocious weather, she was pulled free by her sister "Northella" commanded by Skipper Ted Fox. Earlier a nine man salavage team, led by Skipper Charles Drever, had boarded Junella from a boat and attached a tow line.

When she had been towed clear of the Minches, Junella proceeded to Stornaway under her own power, with Northella standing by. This fine feat of seamanship had saved Junella from a notorious graveyard of wrecks. Skipper Drever's salvage team was made up of Bill Seymour, 2nd officer (Northella), 3 deck hands (Northella), Cyril Clark Ch. Eng. (Northella), Colin Nichol, owners' Asst. Marine Eng. and 2 representatives of the UK Trawlers Mutual Ins. Co. Ltd.

The Harbourmaster refused permission to enter Stornaway harbour as he was worried the Junella might sink and block the harbour. Skipper Drever took her in, however, and later she came back to Hull for repairs.

Junella served as a minesweeper in the Falklands conflict, 11th April 1982 till 20th October 1982.

In July 1983 Junella was sold to Greenland owners but in 1987 she has been bought back by Stan Marr for fishing in the Falklands area.

Now Hillcove
X Vesttral 1987
X Siku 1985
X Junella 1983

KIRKELLA

Kirkella ran her fishing trials in the North Sea off Aberdeen at the end of June 1965. For her maiden voyage Skipper Drever took Kirkella to the Newfoundland grounds, sailing from Hull on the 1st July 1965. On her return after 36 days she landed 479 tonnes 18cwt., mainly cod from a 39 day trip. From her 2nd trip Kirkella set up a national record catch of 550 tonnes, mainly of cod from a 39 day trip to Greenland.

In 1967 the White Fish Authority chartered Kirkella for an exploratory fishing trip to the coasts of Angola and S.W.

Name	Reg. No.	Off. No.	Tons	Length/ Breadth	Call Sign
Kirkella	H 367	305792	1714	245.6	GQSU
			694	40.6	

Builder	Type
Hall Russell & Co.Ltd. Aberdeen 1965	Wholefish Freezer

Factory Details

28,000 cu.ft. fish hold
11 x 12 Station L. Sterne V.P. freezers capable of freezing 25 tons per day.

Engine Details

English Electric Co.
Diesel Electric
3 x Type CSKPRM
3237 BHP 15½ knots

Launched	Skipper Maiden Voyage	Crew No.
8th July 1964	Charles Drever	24

Named by

Mrs G. Edwards Marr, wife of the Chairman of J. Marr & Son

By 1984 Kirkella was the last of the J. Marr freezer trawlers to remain in the fishing role, until she was sold for standby work to Seaboard Offshore Ltd. Inverness. Of the 10 J. Marr freezers, 4 were sold for fishing to foreign owners, 2 were sold for standby work and 4 are in J. Marr's survey fleet.

Now Seabord Implacable, standby safety and firefighting vessel.
X Kirkella 1984

MARBELLA

Marbella ran her trials off the Humber on the 21st April. She sailed on her maiden voyage on the 28th April, commanded by Skipper Charles Drever, who took Marbella fishing in the Canadian fishing grounds. She returned home after 48 days, on the 15th June 1966, to set up a new national record catch of 613 tonnes.

Africa. Kirkella, commanded by Skipper Drever, sailed from Hull on the 18th October 1967. During the trip she steamed around 12,000 miles and returned to Hull on the 16th December 1967, with 100 tonnes of fish in frozen fillets, consisting of hake, king klip, bream, snoek and horse mackerel, for assessment of commercial values and retention of quality after being frozen.

Name	Reg. No.	Off. No.	Tons	Length/ Breadth	Call Sign
Marbella	H 384	308539	1786	254.6	GRZE
			718	40.7	

Builder	Type
Goole S.B. & R. Co.	Wholefish
Goole 1966	Freezer

Factory Details

30,000 cu.ft. fish hold
14 x 12 Station L. Sterne V.P. Freezers able to freeze 600 kits per day in 90lb blocks

Engine Details

English Electric
Diesel Electric
2 x Type 12 CVSM
3506 BHP 15 knots

Launched	Skipper Maiden Voyage	Crew No.
26th October 1965	Charles Drever	24

Named by

Mrs Hilda Hogan, wife of Arthur T. Hogan, Chief Superintendent Engineer for the owners.

On her second voyage, from a 42 day trip to Newfoundland in which she steamed an estimated 7,000 miles, Marbella landed in Hull on the 3rd August 1966, beating her previous record by 69 tonnes to set up a new record of 642 tonnes, of mainly cod and 1 ton of halibut.

Having set up 2 national records in 1966, Marbella went on to become top British freezer in 1967, landing 3,784 tonnes, equal to 60,544 kits.

In November 1966 whilst homeward bound from Newfoundland Marbella answered the distress call of the motor vessel Kathar, a 1247 ton coaster. The stricken vessel was drifting on to Cape Wrath. It took Marbella 90 minutes to fight through the ensuing gale to reach Kathar and put a line on her, by which time she was only 2 miles off Cape Wrath, and had the local lifeboat standing by, to take off the crew. Marbella kept the Kathar in tow for $1\frac{1}{2}$ hours whilst her engines were repaired and she was able to proceed on her way to port. Marbella arrived in Hull and landed her catch of 372 tonnes for 43 days.

On the 2nd March 1977 whilst fishing off the Norwegian coast, Marbella trawled up a lifeboat cover, which had

Photo by courtesy of Steve Pulfrey.

identification marks of being from the ill-fated Gaul.

Whilst outward bound to the Norwegian coast on the 25th January 1978 Marbella's engine room caught fire, due to an overflow of oil onto a hot surface. This was put out by flooding the engine room with CO_2. She was towed into Aalesund by the Norwegian rescue vessel, Hjalmar Bjoerjke, but was able to return to Hull under her own power where she arrived on the 2nd February for repairs. No-one was injured.

In 1978 Marbella was converted to standby work, and on the 22nd October 1979 she sailed to Middlesbrough to be converted for survey work. She was given the new name Northern Horizon, but is still owned by J. Marr and Son.

Now Northern Horizon
X Marbella 1979 - Seismographic survey vessel.

Origin of Name

Second J. Marr trawler to use the name. The other was the big sidewinder H52 built in 1955 at Beverley and sold in 1965 to Boyd Line.

NORTHELLA (1)

Northella arrived in her home port of Hull on the 29th September 1964 after running fishing trials in the North Sea off Aberdeen on the 15th September 1964.

On her maiden voyage to Newfoundland and Labrador, Skipper Drever found fishing to be slack. Northella steamed 7,000 miles during the trip and at one point she was

Name	Reg. No.	Off. No.	Tons	Length/ Breadth	Call Sign
Northella (1)	H 301	305762	1718	254.6	GNCE
			696	40.6	

Builder	Type
Hall Russell & Co. Ltd. Aberdeen 1964	Wholefish Freezer

Factory Details

28,000 cu.ft. fish hold
14 x 12 Station L. Sterne V.P. freezers
Capable of freezing 37 tons per day

Engine Details

English Electric Co.
Diesel Electric
Type 8 CSRKM
2700 BHP

Launched	Skipper Maiden Voyage	Crew No.
8th July 1964	Charles Drever	26

Named by

Mrs G. Alan Marr, wife of a Director of the owners

only 350 miles off New York. In 22 days of actual fishing she caught 311 tonnes 18 cwt: 278 cod, 14 haddock, 19 dabs, 13cwt. coley, 3cwt. halibut and 2cwt. catfish, landing back in Hull after 42 days. But in better fishing days in June 1965 she landed a British record of 507 tonnes of codstuffs.

In the winter of 1965, as Northella trawled through a blizzard in the Newfoundland grounds, the Officer of the Watch asked the bridge lookouts to watch for an approaching radar echo. Suddenly, out of the gloom of the driving snow appeared the ghostly shape of a sailing ship, causing a chill to run down the spine of the port lookout. What he must have glimpsed was an old 5 masted schooner which was a Portuguese Dory mother ship and was in the area at this time.

In the early hours of the 15th January 1966 Northella sailed from Hull bound for Newfoundland. At 1.35 a.m. as a snow storm was sweeping across the Humber she crashed through the Regent oil jetty at Killingholme. The impact caused great damage to the jetty and caused Skipper Townend to fall overboard. Luckily he was safely picked up suffering from exposure. A concrete base had holed Northella and her engine room began to flood, so at 1.40 a Mayday was sent out. Immediately the Immingham based tug, Lady Theresa, answered the call and came to Northella's aid, coming alongside at 2.14 a.m. She began to tow her

to Immingham, but with the engine room flooded and water still pouring in she was in danger of sinking. It was decided the only safe course was to beach her until pumps could be put on board. Lady Theresa then took off 26 crew men and landed them at Immingham. By the 17th January Northella had been safely refloated and was in Immingham graving dock ready for repairs. Except for 2 cases of exposure, no-one was injured in the incident.

In 1973 Northella sailed to Cape Town to be converted to fish the southern ocean grounds of the Falklands, South Georgia and British Arctic waters, for her new owners, the Atlantic Trawling Pty, of Hout Bay, South Africa. She was renamed Yellow Fin and was later joined by the former Junella, then named Blue Fin.

Now Southern Fighter, still fishing and registered at Georgetown, Cayman Islands
X Yellow Fin 1977
X Northella 1973

Photo by courtesy of Peter Horsley.

NORTHELLA (2)

The Northella was delivered on the 26th November 1973 and sailed direct from the Tyne on her maiden voyage 2 days later. She was commanded by Skipper Ted Fox who took Northella to the White Sea grounds, but after 3 weeks with problems she returned to Hull. Repairs were held up over the Christmas holidays and she returned to sea on the 6th January 1974. Skipper Fox returned to the N.E. Atlantic grounds and after a successful trip she landed back in

Name	Reg. No.	Off. No.	Tons	Length/Breadth	Call Sign
Northella (2)	H 206	362208	1238	230.4	GTIW
			441	41.8	

Builder	Type
Clelands Shipbuilding Co.Ltd. Wallsend 1973	Wholefish Freezer

Factory Details

35,000 cu.ft. fish hold
10 x 20 Station Jackstone Froster V.P. Freezers, capable of freezing 46 tons per day in 100lb blocks
Type 28 Shetland Gutter
Cold Liver Oil plant 3 boilers

Engine Details

Mirrlees Blackstone
Type KMR Major 7
3246 BHP 16½ knots

Launched	Skipper Maiden Voyage	Crew No.
2nd July 1973	Ted Fox	24

Named by

Mrs M. Hunter, Sister-in law of Mr. Andrew L. Marr, Director of J. Marr

Hull on the 12th April, with 549.8 tonnes of blocks of good quality fish.

The reason for going to the North East grounds instead of the traditional freezer grounds of Newfoundland and Labrador was that large shoals of swaddies (redfish) were being found there which were unsuitable for the British Market.

In 1977 Northella, with Skipper Ted Fox, towed the Farnella under Skipper A. Powdrill home from Little Hoy Norway, a distance of 1,000 miles. Farnella had developed problems with her variable pitch propeller. Due to the high cost of such a tow trawlers in trouble usually arranged a tow with a homeward bound British trawler or even better a ship from the same Company. The towing vessel's crew would be paid "salvage money" about a year later.

Northella's best fishing year was 1978 when she was 3rd in the Dolphin Bowl Competition, landing 4579 tonnes. The only trawlers to beat her were Boyd Line's large sister trawlers. So this was an outstanding achievement.

On the 1st October 1980 Northella went to the aid of the stricken Junella which was aground on rocks in the Minches off the Hebrides, Scotland. In a fine feat of seamanship

which included all Northella's crew with Skipper Ted Fox, the Junella was pulled free and as Northella stood by her, was safely taken into Stornaway by Skipper Charles Drever. Northella served as a minesweeper in the South Atlantic during the Falklands War, from the 11th April 1982 when she sailed to Rosyth for conversion until the 19th November when she was returned to her owners.

In July 1983 with no fishing opportunities for British Freezers, Northella was chartered by Trinity House as a guard ship for electrical power cable laying operations in the English Channel, between England and France. Then in October 1983 Northella rejoined the Navy. She was chartered by the M.O.D. for escort and training duties based at the Clyde. Now in 1988 she is based at Portsmouth and painted grey. She is fitted with a decompression chamber and inflatable work boat.

Northella now Training Ship R.N.

This Northella is the 5th J. Marr ship to receive the name the others being:-

H 244: 1946-1948 Built Selby 1946
H 159: 1951-1956 Built Beverley 1951
H 98: 1958-1963 Built Beverley 1958
H 301: 1964-1973 Built Aberdeen 1964

SOUTHELLA

On delivery, Southella was the largest British trawler in length and breadth. She sailed from the builder's yard at Aberdeen on the 6th February 1969 and arrived at her home port of Hull the next day to become the port's 7th

Name	Reg. No.	Off. No.	Tons	Length/ Breadth	Call Sign
Southella	H 40	334106	1144	246.0	MZUR
			382	41.8	

Builder	Type
Hall Russell & Co. Aberdeen 1969	Wholefish Freezer

Factory Details
32,000 cu.ft. fish hold
8 x 20 Station Jackstone Froster V.P. Freezers capable of freezing 50 tons per day

Engine Details
Mirrlees National
Type KMR 8 Major
2880 BHP 16½ knots

Launched	Skipper Maiden Voyage	Crew No.
27th September 1968	Charles Drever	26

Named by
Mrs Evelyn M. Mackenzie, wife of a Director of J. Marr and Son

freezer. She sailed on her maiden voyage on the 13th February commanded by Skipper Charles Drever.

He took Southella fishing at Newfoundland and from a very successful 52 day trip landed 666 tonnes, just 14 tonnes short of breaking the 680 tonne British record held by St. Jerome.

Southella was the top British freezer in 1971. Commanded by Skipper Alfred Eagles she caught 2,574 tonnes of fish in 335 days at sea.

Southella's fine hull design was used by the Royal Navy for their Castle Class Fishery Patrol vessels. Because of her size and speed Southella in May 1976 was chartered to protect the British trawlers at Iceland, with Skipper Ches Abbey.

In the summer of 1980 in an attempt to try to get fish from new areas, Southella sailed into the Baltic to klondyke Baltic cod from Polish trawlers. She returned after 28 days with 666 tonnes of blocks and as this proved to be her last fishing trip, by coincidence she landed the same tonnage on her first and last trips. Her Skipper, Howard Peterson, had been her regular Skipper for 7 years.

In July 1980 Southella was chartered by the Department of Agriculture and Fisheries, Scotland, for fishing patrol and surveillance duties based at Leith for 5 months. This was due to the patrol ship Switha, running aground in the Firth of Forth and having to be blown up.

In January 1981 Southella went to Immingham to be converted to a seismographic survey vessel and J. Marr and Son renamed her Seisella, until 1986 when, chartered by the Falklands Islands, she became the Falklands Desire.

Now Falklands Desire seismographic vessel
X Seisella 1986
X Southella 1981

SWANELLA

Swanella ran her trials off the Humber on the 31st January 1967. She became J. Marr's 5th freezer. Commanded by Skipper Charles Drever, she sailed from Hull on the 3rd February for the Newfoundland fishing grounds. Half-way through the trip Swanella suffered a fractured crank shaft, which reduced her engine power by 50%. This proved to be inadequate to tow her trawl efficiently and so she was brought home early, arriving back in Hull on the 27th March landing a catch of 447 tonnes.

In 1967 Swanella with Skipper Drever set up a new record catch of 665.5 tonnes, mainly of Newfoundland cod. In 1969 Swanella was J. Marr's top trawler landing an impressive 4,105 tonnes of fish for 307 days at sea, only 65 tonnes behind top freezer Lady Parkes which received a place in the Guinness Book of Records.

In August 1972 Swanella was used for a cooking experiment with reheated prepacked frozen meals and microwave ovens. This experiment was doomed to fail, as it left the crew without the timeless privilege of complaining about the cook's shipboard prepared food, which usually was of good quality.

In August 1973 Swanella was chartered by the White

Photo by courtesy of Walter Fussey & Son.

Name	Reg. No.	Off. No.	Tons	Length/Breadth	Call Sign
Swanella	H 421	308571	1779	247.9	GVLU
			714	40.8	

Builder	Type
Goole S.B. & R. Co.	Wholefish
Goole 1967	Freezer

Factory Details

30,000 cu.ft. fish hold
14 x 12 Station L. Sterne V.P. Freezers capable of freezing 600 kits per day in 90lb blocks

Engine Details

English Electric Co.
Diesel Electric
2 x Type 12 CUSM
3506 BHP 15 knots

Launched	Skipper Maiden Voyage	Crew No.
17th October 1966	Charles Drever	24

Named by

Mrs E. Stirk, Mother-in-law of Mr. G. Alan Marr, Director of owners

Fish Authority for a 55 day deep-water exploration trip in the North East Atlantic with special gear and 10 scientists. In October she brought back 80 tonnes of relatively obscure fish, caught between 300-700 fathoms in an arc between West Ireland and the Faroes. The popular press reported the catch as "Monsters of the Deep".

The search for new species never proved successful due to the British housewife's reluctance to change from traditional seafoods.

On the morning of the 8th February Swanella's watchkeepers were the last British crew to see the Gaul before she disappeared.

H 421 Swanella is often confused with the training ship Sir Walter Raleigh, which is in fact the trawler "Hamburg" built in 1965 which was renamed Swanella when acquired by J. Marr for survey work in 1982. She became Sir Walter Raleigh in 1984.

In June 1981 Swanella was sold to Norwegian owners for salvage work, registered at Bodo. In 1982 she was engaged in recovering valuables from the wreck of the Lusitania off the Irish coast. Among items recovered was a bronze propeller and the ship's bell.

Now Drive Performer, diving support ship for offshore installations.
X Archimedes 1985
X Swanella 1981

Photo by courtesy of Steve Pulfrey.

NEWINGTON TRAWLERS

Newington Steam Trawling Co. Ltd., was founded in 1912 by a number of shareholders, including Cochranes of Selby. This Company took its name from the Newington Ward in which St. Andrew's Dock is situated. In the 1920's Henry Burton became manager and major shareholder. He was followed into the Company by his son, also Henry Burton, who became Chairman. By the 1930's the Company was operating 7 deep sea trawlers, some of which went into Naval service in 1939.

After the 1939-45 War through the early 1950's the Company operated 4 ships. In 1953 Michael Burton, Henry Burton senior's grandson, left the Royal Navy to work in Lord Lines offices, managed by Thomas W. Boyd, leaving in 1954 to join his father at Newington. In 1963 Michael Burton succeeded his father as Chairman and Managing Director. In 1968 the Company became Newington Trawlers Ltd.

Through the 1960's the Company's sidewinder Somerset Maugham dominated the Silver Cod Competition, followed in the 1970's by the Company's 2 Wet Fish Stern Trawlers, which were also highly successful. But in the late 1970's with the loss of the deep-sea grounds Newington moved into inshore and North Sea fishing. The Company is still in existence, run by Michael Burton.

NAME THEME: Famous authors.
FUNNEL: Black top, blue with broad grey band.
HULL: Black with white line.

SEAFRIDGE LTD.

Seafridge was a company formed by Mapleship of Canada and the Gadus Company of Norway. The trawlers were placed under the British flag and managed by Newington Trawlers, Hull, whose livery they carried.

NAME THEME: Seafridge prefix with seabirds.

C.S. FORESTER

The C.S. Forester ran her trials off the Humber on the 22nd August 1969. Her Commander was Skipper Bill Brettell, who was first made Skipper in 1960 and won the Silver Cod 4 times in the next 8 years in the sidewinder Somerset Maugham. The C.S. Forester sailed from Hull on her maiden voyage on the 24th August 1969 for the White Sea grounds. During her 19 day trip she encountered slack fishing with hauls of 30-40 baskets, the best being 200 baskets. Also she had trouble with the starboard warp stretching. On her return to Hull her catch of 1681 kits of good quality, shelved fish sold for £7,440.

On the 10th November 1970 whilst outward bound for Spitzbergen fishing grounds, C.S. Forester was in a position about 200 miles off Tromso when at 2 p.m. a fire broke out in her engine room. This was due to fuel spurting onto hot pipes whilst a blocked filter was being changed. On ensuring the engine room was abandoned Skipper Bill Brettell flooded it with CO_2 gas. The 2nd engineer, Cook and galley

Mrs. June Morrison, flanked by Mr. Michael Morrison (left), Director of Seafridge Ltd. and Mr. Anders M. Liaaen (right), Managing Director of A.M. Liaaen A/S, at the launching of the "Seafridge Osprey"

The "Seafridge Osprey" leaves the slipway.

Name	Reg. No.	Off. No.	Tons	Length/Breadth	Call Sign
C.S. Forester	H 86	337325	768	185.7	GZMA
			247	36.1	

Builder	Type
Charles D. Holmes & Co. Beverley 1969	Fresher

Factory Details

16,500 cu.ft. fish hold
1st British Deep Sea trawler to have a type 28 Shetland Gutting machine

Engine Details

Stork - Workspoor
Type TMABF 398 Diesel
1980 BHP 14 knots

Launched	Skipper Maiden Voyage	Crew No.
15th April 1969	Bill Brettell	19

Named by

Miss Ghislaine Burton, daughter of Mr. Michael Burton, Chairman of owners.

boy who were sheltering in the galley from smoke and fumes managed to reach the outer deck safely.

The injured 2nd engineer was lifted off by a Norwegian helicopter and taken to hospital, while the Ross Valiant arrived on the scene and took the stricken C.S. Forester in tow to Harstad. C.S. Forester arrived back in Hull on the 22nd November 1970 after being towed home by a Norwe-

gian salvage tug, the tow taking 9 days. After repairs she returned to sea in January 1971.

The C.S. Forester went on to become Britains, most successful wet fish trawler under Skippers Bill Brettell and later Dick Taylor, although she did have problems in that, although she moved well when fishing, while steaming she steered badly and her stern tended to yaw. This was due to a design fault with her rudder which actually fell off on two occasions: during 1972 after fishing off Skaven, Norway and catching 400 kits of coley Skipper Bill Brettell decided to take the C.S. Forester to Malangen, but after she started steaming her rudder wouldn't respond and she ran in a circle. On inspecting the steering flat it was discovered her rudder had fallen off. After being towed home she was

Photo by courtesy of Walter Fussey & Son.

given the rudder off the Hammond Innes which was being built at Beverley. Then on the 22nd January 1973 C.S. Forester left Hull for a trip to the Barents Sea. Three days later whilst off Andanes she was running before a severe gale when at 18.30 hours as Skipper Dick Taylor was having his evening meal, suddenly the ship started to broach to. The Skipper dashed to the bridge to find the Mate trying her on hand steering, but with no response from the rudder. On inspecting the steering flat, he found water was flooding through the hole left where the rudder should have been. After shipboard repairs she was towed home by the Joseph Conrad with Skipper Dennis Cawood, arriving in Hull on the 31 January 1973. A shipping expert was called in to rectify the fault and after she was fitted with a series of fins near her stern, the problem was cured.

C.S. Forester, with regular Skipper Dick Taylor, was Champion British Trawler in 1976-77-78 and winner of the Hull Challenge Shield. In 1976 she earned £692,822 for 27,600 kits and in 1977 £740,262 for 24,871 kits. In May 1977 Skipper Taylor set up a new British record for a 20 day trip to Bear Island of £92,453 for 2984 kits, followed in May 1978 by a new record of £92,458 for 3052 kits for a 23 day trip to the Norwegian coast. Skipper Dick Taylor earned the nickname "Old Fox" because of his uncanny ability to find fish.

By 1980 the British Deep Sea trawler fleet was in ruins and it was ironic that the C.S. Forester on the 30th April was sold to the "Old Enemy" Iceland, the country which had been most responsible for putting her crew on the dole. She was bought by Agust Sigurdsson, renamed Ran and registered at Hafnarfjordur, Iceland.

Now Solbakur fishing from Akureyri, Iceland
X Dagstjarnan
X Ran 1981
X C.S. Forester

HAMMOND INNES

Name	Reg. No.	Off. No.	Tons	Length/ Breadth	Call Sign
Hammond Innes	H 180	359149	897	191.0	GQHV
			306	37.1	

Builder	Type
Charles D. Holmes & Co. Beverley 1972	Fresher

Factory Details

19,500 cu.ft. Fishroom lined with 2″ thick redwood.
Temp 32°F.
2 Type 28 Shetland Gutters

Engine Details

Stork - Werkspoor
Type 6TM 410 6 cyl.
2500 BHP 14 knots

Launched	Skipper Maiden Voyage	Crew No.
16th May 1972	Bill Brettell	15

Named by

Mrs Sylvia Nowell, wife of Mr. Nowell, a Director of Newingtons

Due to the success of the C.S. Forester, Newington Trawlers decided to have built a larger trawler of a similar design. The Hammond Innes ran her trials on the 20th January 1973. She was commanded by Skipper Bill Brettell who was nicknamed the "Bear Island Ghost" due to his habit of fishing in remote areas with difficult ground, gullies and ledges. Also a lone trawler which found a fish shop could have several days good fishing, whereas a number of trawlers working on fish would soon limit the catching ability. Hence the preference of trawlers to keep to radio silence so as not to let the opposition know where they were.

The Hammond Innes sailed from Hull on the 29th January 1973 and from a 24 day trip to the Norwegian Coast landed 1892 kits on the 22nd February grossing £25,739. On her second trip, 7 days after she left Hull her engines broke down and she had to put into Harstad for repairs. Her 9 day stay meant her catch of 645 kits had to be discharged and sold for £3,915. After repairs she was able to resume fishing and after being away for a total of 39 days the Hammond Innes arrived back in Hull on the 9th April where her catch of 2,467 kits sold for a world record price of £38,108.

In her brief career of only 4 years the Hammond Innes was highly successful, being winner of the Hull Challenge Shield, in 1974 landing 31,275 kits (Skipper Bill Brettell) and in 1975 landing 36,702 kits (Skipper Dick Taylor). In 1976 she was runner up, a month languishing in dry dock on the Tyne spoiling her chance of winning the Shield even though Skipper Brettell set up a world record of £89,876 in December 1976.

Most stern trawler owners were happy with the contract price of fish paid to freezers rather than the gamble of the wet fish market and the foreign market. In 1974 during a trip to Spitzbergen Hammond Innes had to call into Aalesund for repairs, but once she began fishing, in only 10 days, she filled her fishroom full of top class cod, a catch estimated at over 5,000 kits. Due to a bobbers' strike at Hull she was diverted to Cuxhaven in Germany. Her catch took 2 days to unload during which time, some of the crew became troublesome due to drinking. A discrepancy occurred of over 1,000 kits lower, being credited as landed, and the trip only grossed £47,700. 3 days later Somerset Maugham landed at Hull with 3,000 kits and made £60,000.

On the 13th December 1977 the Hammond Innes was sold to Canadian interests for conversion into a fishery research vessel asnd renamed "Lady Hammond", after the wife of Sir Andrew Snape Hammond who was Lieutenant Governor of Nova Scotia, 1780-1782.

Photo by courtesy of Walter Fussey & Son.

Now Lady Hammond Canadian research vessel.
X Hammond Innes 1977.

World Record Trips By The Hammond Innes - under Skipper Bill Brettell

April 1973: £38,108 for 2,467 kits, 24 days Norwegian coast
December 1973: £50,450 for 2,598 kits, 22 days White Sea
(First trawler to break £50,000 barrier).
February 1974: £73,216 for 4,501 kits, 22 days Norwegian coast.
December 1976: £89,874 for 2,822 kits, 28 days Bear Island.

SEAFRIDGE OSPREY

Seafridge Osprey was delivered to her owners on the 26th April 1972. She sailed direct from the builder's yard during May for her maiden voyage, and Skipper Cawood took her to fish at the Norwegian coast and White Sea grounds. She arrived at her home port of Hull for the first time on the 13th August 1972, landing 364 tonnes of plaice and haddock, 238 tonnes in fillets, the rest whole, a catch equal to 911.4 tonnes wholefish. The weather for the 88 day trip had been good, but the fishing had been very patchy and slack.

She sailed for her second voyage on the 24th August 1972 with Skipper Malcolm Meadows in command, as Dennis Cawood was taking over the next new ship.

On the 20th March 1973 Seafridge Osprey, commanded by Skipper Graham Wilson, was in Harstad for engine repairs, when at 7 p.m. a fire swept through the bridge and forward accommodation. 2nd mate, John Harvey was trap-

Name	Reg. No.	Off. No.	Tons	Length/ Breadth	Call Sign
Seafridge Osprey	H 137	342739	879	197.0	GPOG
			357	36.2	

Builder	Type
A.M. Liaaen A/S Aalesund 1972	Factory Freezer

Factory Details	Baader Equipment
600 tons fish hold 2 Drammen H.P. Freezers Able to freeze 24 tons per day.	2 Production lines Type 419 Header Type 98 Filleter Type 338 Filleter Type 46 Skinner Type 47 Skinner

Engine Details
Burmeister & Wain Type 1226 MBTF - 40V 2160 BHP 14½ knots

Launched	Skipper Maiden Voyage	Crew No.
4th March 1972	Dennis Cawood	33

Named by
Mrs June Morrison, wife of Mr. Michael Morrison, M.D. of Seafridge Ltd.

ped in his cabin by the smoke and flames but he managed to smash a port hole, and was handed a water hose and oxygen mask by the Harstad firemen as they battled to free him. He sprayed himself with the water to minimise the heat then covered himself with a tarpaulin as he was dragged clear of the burning ship, through a hole cut by the firemen.

On the 15th April, Seafridge Osprey was towed back to Hull by the Hull tug Tradesman, and inspected by forensic scientists to find out the cause of the fire. She also landed 200 tonnes of undamaged fillets. On the 1st August a Norwegian tug took her back to her builder's yard for repairs as they had quoted a lower price than any British yard.

After a very short life as a Hull trawler, Seafridge Osprey was sold to Norwegian owners, the Gadus Company in 1975. In 1982 she was converted into a survey vessel.

Now Geco Sigma, Norwegian seismographic survey vessel.
X Svalbard 1982
X Gadus III 1977
X Seafridge Osprey 1975

SEAFRIDGE PETREL

Name	Reg. No.	Off. No.	Tons	Length/ Breadth	Call Sign
Seafridge Petrel	H 175	359170	878	196.9	GRUV
			357	36.2	

Builder	Type
A.M. Liaaen A/S Aalesund 1973	Factory Freezer

Factory Details	Baader Equipment
600 tons fish hold 2 Drammen H.P. Freezers Able to freeze 24 tons per day	2 production lines Type 419 Header Type 99 Filleter Type 338 Filleter Type 46 Skinner Type 47 Skinner

Engine Details
Burmeister and Wain Type 1226 MBTF - 40v 2160 BHP 14½ knots

Launched	Skipper Maiden Voyage	Crew No.
17th February 1973	Dennis Cawood	33

Named by
Mrs Diane Lovell, wife of Mr Peter Lovell, of Brekkes Group Ltd. Hull

Seafridge Petrel was delivered to her owners on the 31st March 1973 and like her sisters sailed directly to the fishing grounds on her maiden voyage. Due to slack fishing, Skipper Cawood had to take her fishing at the White Sea, Bear Island and Spitzbergen, arriving back in Hull with 400 tonnes of fish both in fillets and whole fish after a trip of 90 days.

In 1975 Seafridge Petrel caught an estimated 2,466 tonnes, finishing 9th in the Dolphin Bowl Competition, and in 1976 2,050 tonnes. During her brief career she set up a British record with skipper Dennis Cawood of 550 tonnes of fillets, equal to 1830 tonnes wholefish landed from one trip.

On her last trip she arrived at Hull on the 1st July 1977 landing 295 tonnes of fillets and 145 tonnes of wholefish from the White Sea and Bear Island, sailing finally from Hull on the 27th July 1977. Thus after 5 years the last of the 3 ships had transferred to the Gadus Co. Norway, their chance of making a living under the British flag ruined by quotas and traditional fish grounds being made off-limits to foreign trawlers.

Now B.C.M. Atlantic fishing from Halifax N.S. Canada.
X Sea Petrel 1980
X Gadus II 1979
X Seafridge Petrel 1977

SEAFRIDGE SKUA

The hull of the Seafridge Skua was built at Hasund Hek Verksted and after her launch at Hasund she was completed at Aalesund. She was delivered to her owners on the 9th September 1972 and sailed on her maiden voyage direct from the builder's yard on the 24th September 1972, commanded by Skipper D. Cawood. She fished the Norwegian coast and White Sea grounds, arriving in Hull after 90 days and landing 400 tonnes of fish, 254 tonnes of which were fillets. 870 tonnes of wholefish would be needed to produce the fillets.

On her second voyage she sailed to Greenland and on the 20th January 1973 became the first British trawler to be allowed into Iceland for 4½ months, to land a sick crewman at Reykjavik, this being due to the hostilities between the British and Icelandic governments in the cod war. The local doctor and the Seafridge's Skipper were able to break down the barrier of ill-will, the life of the crewman being much more important.

On the 1st October 1974 the Hull Fire Brigade was called to attend the Seafridge Skua at Hull Fish Dock. Her engine room had flooded to a depth of 8 feet and firemen spent several hours pumping her out. Engineers then began to

Name	Reg. No.	Off. No.	Tons	Length/ Breadth	Call Sign
Seafridge Skua	H 138	359137	878 357	196.9 36.2	MVOE

Builder	Type
A.M. Liaaen A/S Aalesund 1972	Factory Freezer

Factory Details	Baader Equipment
600 tons fish hold 2 Drammen H.P.Freezers Able to freeze 24 tons per day	2 production lines Type 419 Header Type 99 Filleter Type 338 Filleter Type 46 Skinner Type 47 Skinner

Engine Details

Burmeister & Wain
Type 1226 MBTF 40v.
2160 BHP 14½ knots

Launched	Skipper Maiden Voyage	Crew No.
3rd March 1972	Dennis Cawood	33

Named by

Miss Jeanet Webster, engaged to Michael Burton, Manager of Newington Trawlers Ltd.

trawlers, Seafridge Skua was sold to Gadus of Norway on the 12th May 1976 after sailing out of Hull for only 3 years. She is still fishing from Norway and revisited Hull in June 1988.

Now Ramoen, Aalesund, Norway, Reg. No. M-2-VD
X Vartdal Viking 1977
X Gadus 1977
X Seafridge 1976

investigate the reason for this flooding. The trawler had been tied up for 2 weeks at the time of the mishap. She was able to sail from Hull on the 3rd October, after the fault was rectified.

Due to quotas being introduced, badly affecting British

RANGER FISHING COMPANY

In the 1960's the old established trawling firm Purdy Trawlers Ltd. of North Shields approached the P & O Shipping Company, with a plan for a fleet of factory trawlers that would feed into one of P & O's refridgerated cargo ships. As a result the Ranger Fishing Company was formed in 1965, with Mr. John F. Purdy as Chairman and Purdy Trawlers as managers.

Brooke Marine, the Lowestoft shipbuilders, built 3 small revolutionary factory trawlers, with the assistance of the Torry Research Institute of Aberdeen who gave advice. The 3 trawlers however never worked with a cargo ship as was planned.

As the local fishermen were mainly engaged in near-water fishing, the Ranger Fishing Co. recruited 3 experienced deep-water Skippers from Hull, Freddy Grey, Les Abbey and John Dobson. Experienced Humberside crews were also taken on.

In 1970 to expand the operation 2 large West German factory trawlers were acquired, and 4 more factory trawlers were ordered from Brook Marine for delivery between 1971-72.

In 1973 during a time of intense competition between shipping companies for cargos, resulting in low freight rates, P & O Shipping Company had to reorganise its shipping operations and decided to sell its 8 Ranger trawlers. These were acquired by British United Trawlers and moved to Hull during August 1973.

NAME THEME: Characters from Greek Mythology.
FUNNEL: Lower part pale green with house flag, above which were 2 black bands separated by a white band.
HULL: Lower dark green, upper pale green.

RANGER AJAX

Ranger Ajax was the first of the 3 'A' class trawlers and was lost before the fleet was transferred to B.U.T. ownership.

In 1965 as Ranger Ajax waited off Lowestoft for her crew to join for her fishing trials, the weather deteriorated and the sea became rough. The boat taking out the crew could not risk coming alongside to put her crew on board and had to return to harbour. This was a blessing in disguise as had she tried fishing in heavy seas she could have capsized due to her stern mast being top heavy. This was removed and replaced by rollers on 2 stanchions with 2 turtle blocks.

From a 66 day maiden voyage Ranger Ajax landed 170 tonnes of fillets, equal to 600 tonnes of wholefish. She suffered the usual teething problems.

On her second trip she fished at Greenland and because of the high sea temperature encountered problems with her freezers. She went into St. Johns, Newfoundland, for technical assistance. The locals were amazed to see such a small factory trawler in their waters.

Loss Details

Ranger Ajax was fishing off the south east tip of Greenland, when on the 17th May 1972 around 3.30 a.m a fire broke

Name	Reg. No.	Off. No.	Tons	Length/Breadth	Call Sign
Ranger Ajax	SN 147	187945	778	171.0	GZXH
			333	32.5	

Builder	Type
Brooke Marine Ltd.	Factory
Lowestoft 1965	Freezer

Factory Details	Baader Equipment
13,000 cu.ft.	1 x Header
Jackstone Froster	1 Type 188 Filleter
H.P. Freezer	1 Type 99 Filleter
	1 Type 46 Skinner
	1 Type 47 Skinner

Engine Details

English Electric Co.
Diesel Electric
Type 12 CUSM
1270 BHP 12 knots

Launched	Skipper Maiden Voyage	Crew No.
5th April 1965	Freddy Grey	26

Named by

Mrs J.F. Purdy, wife of Chairman of owners.

out in the food storeroom. Although the crew fought the fire they were unable to control it. Skipper Arthur Ness sent out a Mayday and several ships raced to her aid. The 26 crew men abandoned Ranger Ajax in the ship's life-raft and were picked up by the West German mother ship Frithjof. A boarding party from the Frithjof put a tow line on Ranger Ajax and tried to tow her to safety. But the next morning she began to list to port and eventually she rolled over and sank. All the crew were safely landed at Reykjavik by the German mother ship.

RANGER APOLLO

Ranger Apollo was the second 'A' class trawler. She was delivered in December 1965 to her home port of North Shields and given the Reg. No. SN 148. When she sailed on her maiden voyage she had problems with her engines and had to return to North Shields. After repairs she sailed for the Norwegian fishing grounds, where ports with good repair yards were close at hand. This area was a popular teething ground for new ships.

In early August 1973 Ranger Apollo became the last of the Ranger fleet to land her catch at North Shields, before

Name	Reg. No.	Off. No.	Tons	Length/ Breadth	Call Sign
Ranger Apollo	SN 148	187946	779	171.0	GRMA
Turcoman	H 233		333	32.5	

Builder	Type
Brooke Marine Ltd. Lowestoft 1965	Factory Freezer

Factory Details	Baader Equipment
Fish hold 13,000cu.ft. Jackstone Froster H.P. Freezer	1 Heading Machine 1 Type 188 Filleter 1 Type 99 Filleter 1 Type 46 Skinner 1 Type 47 Skinner

Engine Details

English Electric Co.
Diesel Electric
Type 12 CUSM
1270 BHP 12 knots

Launched	Skipper Maiden Voyage	Crew No.
15th May	Les Abbey	23

Named by

Mrs Mitchell, wife of a director of P. & O.

coming to Hull to join the B.U.T. fleet. On the 15th December she was renamed "Turcoman", a name previously carried by the old Hellyer sidewinder H 163 between 1937 and 1948.

Because of the limited quotas of fish each British company was allowed to catch, B.U.T. gave preference to the

the more modern vessels. Turcoman was rarely used and spent most of the time laid up. On the 17th May 1977.she was sold for standby work in the oil industry.

Now Port King
X Putford Protector 1987
X Kilsyth 1983
X Turcoman 1977
X Ranger Apollo 1973

RANGER AURORA

Ranger Aurora was the third ship in her class. She was delivered in February 1966 and allotted the fishing number SN 149. She was fitted with water stabilizer tanks which worked against the roll of the ship, in that as the ship rolled to port the water ran to starboard to neutralise the roll, and vice versa. These were never a success on small ships and on

Name	Reg. No.	Off. No.	Tons	Length/Breadth	Call Sign
Ranger Aurora	SN 149	187947	780	171.0	GRQE
Esquimaux	H 236		334	32.5	

Builder	Type
Brooke Marine Ltd. Lowestoft 1966	Factory Freezer

Factory Details	Baader Equipment
13,000 cu.ft. Jackstone Froster H.P. Freezer	1 Header 1 Type 188 Filleter 1 Type 99 Filleter 1 Type 46 Skinner 1 Type 47 Skinner

Engine Details
English Electric Diesel Electric Type 12 CUSM 1270 BHP 12 knots

Launched	Skipper Maiden Voyage	Crew No.
29th July 1965	John Dobson	26

Named by
Mrs M.G.C. Fidler, sister of the Chairman of Ranger Fishing Co.

one occasion caused Ranger Aurora to jerk back violently into a big wave which damaged the plates on her side.

On her second voyage she fished at Greenland. She returned home after a trip of 75 days and landed 203 tonnes of fillets. For this she realised £38,874 (£1.4s. per stone,

1s.8½d per lb, £1.20p per stone, 8½p per lb).

In 1966, while Ranger Aurora was fishing off the Norwegian coast after hauling her trawl on board, a mine was spotted among the fish causing the deck to clear very fast. On closer inspection a brave crewman discovered the mine to be hollow and corroded, and it was dumped back overboard.

In 1973 Ranger Aurora joined the B.U.T. fleet and moved to Hull, when she was renamed Esquimaux. After arriving in Hull she was only rarely used for fishing, and on the 9th May 1977 was sold for standby work.

Now "Grampian Fury" owned by George Craig of Aberdeen as a standby safety and pollution control ship.

X Harlaw 1984
X Esquimaux 1977
X Ranger Aurora 1973

RANGER BOREAS

Name	Reg. No.	Off. No.	Tons	Length/ Breadth	Call Sign
Ranger Boreas	SN 14	338101	1287	242.5	GNIP
Afghan	H 237		534	36.2	

Builder	Type
Rickmers Werft Bremerhaven 1963	Fresher converted to Factory freezer

Factory Details

4 fish holds. Capacity for 325 tons of fillets

Baader Equipment

3 Filleting lines
1. Type 99 Filleter, 412 Header, 46 Skinner (Whitefish)
2. Type 150 Filleter, 47 Skinner (Redfish)
3. Type 338 Filleter, 47 Skinner (small Whitefish)

Engine Details

Maschf. Augsburg - Nurnburg A.G. Diesel Electric
Man. 6 Cyl. Diesel
1500 BHP 15½ knots

Launched	Skipper Maiden Voyage	Crew No.
5th June 1963	Peter Abbey British flag	31

The Ranger Fishing Company bought the "Blankenese" from Partentreederei of Hamburg, Germany, in December 1969 for a sum of £300,000. She was renamed Ranger Boreas and given the registration no: SN 14. At the time she became one of the biggest factory trawlers under the British flag.

On taking command of the ship Skipper Peter Abbey's first job was an urgent request for an English-German dictionary as everything was written in German, to such an extent that when the ship got to sea on her way to the fishing grounds, on opening the medicine locker to treat a sick crewman, the Skipper was surprised to find rows of bottles all in German text.

Early in January 1970 Ranger Boreas sailed for her first British voyage. Skipper Abbey took her to the Norwegian fishing grounds. She proved to be a good ship and after a spell of good fishing the quota of fillets was caught. As there was still some room left in the fishrooms and good fishing available, Skipper Abbey took the Ranger Boreas to Honningsvaag to take on a supply of crushed ice. On returning to the grounds a further 1200 kits of fresh fish were caught for the North Shields market.

In the summer of 1970 Ranger Boreas was fishing at the Barents Sea. Whilst towing on a calm flat sea she suddenly

lurched up in the water. On hauling her gear the doors and Dan Lenos were missing and her bobbins and headline floats were crushed. She had detonated a mine or a bomb on the seabed. She was in a position just to the north of the wreck of H.M.S. Edinburgh at the time. The well constructed Ranger Boreas suffered no damage to her plates and was able to continue fishing.

In 1973 Ranger Boreas became part of the B.U.T. Hull fleet. She was renamed "Afghan", but she was only used for a few trips and on entering Albert Dock on the 2nd August 1975 was permanently laid up, until the 24th November 1979 when she sailed to Blyth for scrapping.

On one of her last voyages, in December 1974 she landed 130 tonnes of fillets at Milford Haven, because of industrial problems at Hull. She had sailed from Hull on the 18th September and had been fishing in the Newfoundland grounds.

RANGER BRISEIS

In 1970 Ranger Fishing Company decided to build up their fleet; to do this two large West German trawlers were bought. The second of these ships was the Fritz Homann bought from Kampf & Co. K.G. of Bremerhaven in June 1970. After slight alterations she began fishing from North Shields. She was renamed "Ranger Briseis" and received the fishing number SN 30. Although she was a fine strong ship her factory equipment was well worn.

In October 1972 during the 2nd cod war, the Board of Trade chartered Ranger Briseis and she was converted into

Name	Reg. No.	Off. No.	Tons	Length/ Breadth	Call Sign
Ranger Briseis	SN 30	338102	1319	250.11	GONW
Hausa			547	36.5	
x Fritz Homann 70					

Builder	Type
Rickmers Werft Bremerhaven 1962	Fresher converted to Factory freezer

Baader Equipment

Line 1: 1 Type 99 Filleter, 1 Type 412 Header, 2 Type 46 Skinners
Line 2: 1 Type 150 Filleter, 2 Type 47 Skinners (Redfish)
Line 3: 1 Type 33 Filleter (Herring)

Engine Details

Klockner-Humboldt-Deutz
2000 BHP 13½ knots

Launched	Skipper Maiden Voyage	Crew No.
12th April 1962 Delivered 30th June 1962	John Dobson British flag	42

a support ship to give medical, weather-communications and advice to the fleet at Iceland, commanded by Peter Durham and Peter Donaghue. From this role she never returned to fishing.

In 1973 with the rest of the Ranger fleet she moved to Hull, having been bought by B.U.T. She was renamed "Hausa" in line with their fleet's tribal names, but as she was no longer fishing she did not receive a registration no.

In 1974 Hausa stood by the C.S. Forester which had been

fired on with live shells and holed by the Icelandic gunboat Thor, but was unable to intervene in the incident.

Hausa was transferred to Grimsby on the 27th April 1977 and then back to Hull on the 3rd May 1979. On the 27th November 1979 she sailed to Blyth for scraping.

RANGER CADMUS

Ranger Cadmus was named by Lady Harmer on the 17th of September 1970, which was the date scheduled for her launch. But due to industrial action being taken by the shipyard workers at her builder's yard she was not launched until the 15th October 1970. Ranger Cadmus was the first of four sisters of the "C" class. Based at North Shields her registration no. became SN 15. She sailed on her maiden voyage in September 1971 to the Norwegian fishing grounds commanded by Skipper John Dobson, who half-way through the trip handed over command to Skipper Peter Abbey (Skipper Dobson returned home to take over the new Ranger Calliope). On her return to North Shields

Name	Reg. No.	Off. No.	Tons	Length/ Breadth	Call Sign
Ranger Cadmus	SN 15	338105	1106	216.9	GOZY
Arab	H 238		411	40.2	

Builder	Type
Brooke Marine Ltd. Lowestoft 1971	Factory Freezer

Factory Details

21,000 cu.ft.
3 White fish fillet lines
1 Red fish fillet line
3 APV Clark H.P. freezer able to freeze 20 tons per day
Shetland type 28 gutter

Baader Equipment

1 type 412 header
2 type 421 headers
1 type 99 filleter
2 type 188 filleters
3 type 47 skinners
1 type 150 fillet/header for red fish

Engine Details

English Electric Ruston Paxman Diesels Ltd.
Type 16 RK3CH Diesel
2600 BHP 13½ knots

Launched	Skipper Maiden Voyage	Crew No.
15th October 1970	John Dobson Peter Abbey	33

Named by

Lady Harmer, wife of the Chairman of P. & O. Lines

after 80 days, Ranger Cadmus landed just over 300 tonnes of fillets.

In 1973 Ranger Cadmus became part of the B.U.T. fleet and moved to Hull. She was renamed Arab. The previous Hull trawler to carry this name was H 293, built for Hellyer Bros. in 1937, which as H.M.T. Arab was commanded by Lt Richard Stannard who won the Victoria Cross at Namsos Norway in April 1940.

In three 80 day trips during 1975-76 on each occasion Arab, commanded by Skipper Peter Abbey, landed over 350 tonnes of fillets, the 1060 tonnes of fillets equal to 3749 tonnes of wholefish. If caught during one year this would have put Arab around the top of the Dolphin Bowl charts. On the last of these trips insufficient 40lb cartons had been placed on board, so the fillets had to be packed in a warehouse ashore.

In early 1977 Arab commanded by Skipper Frank Dre-

wery had to be towed into Honningsvaag by the trawler Dane with Skipper Roy Waller. The two ships tied up alongside each other to await the outcome of repairs, but during the night a severe gale blew up, causing the ships to bang against each other. Dane took up the tow and took Arab down through the shelter of the Fjords to the southern end of Norway from where a Norwegian tug brought Arab home to the Humber.

In August 1981 Arab was sold to Norwegian owners.

Now Pero fishing from Aalesund Reg. No. M-81-VD
X NY Pero 1983
X Arab 1981

RANGER CALLIOPE

Ranger Calliope was the second of a class of four factory trawlers built by Brooke Marine, at a total cost of £3.2 million. Although she was named on the 1st March 1971, due to insufficient water at the shipyard the 'launch' took place a week later when although the shipyard's shipwrights were on a one day protest strike against the proposed Industrial Relations Bill, they went into work without pay to get Ranger Calliope launched.

After running fishing trials in the North Sea, on the 6th March 1972 she sailed from North Shields on her maiden voyage to the Norwegian coast, commanded by Skipper John Dobson.

The main advantage of running maiden voyages off the Norwegian coast was that there were many good ports with repair facilities should problems occur; also Ranger Fishing

Name	Reg. No.	Off. No.	Tons	Length/ Breadth	Call Sign
Ranger Calliope	SN16	338106	1106	216.9	GPAF
Kelt	H 240		411	40.3	

Builder	Type
Brooke Marine Ltd. Lowestoft 1972	Wholefish Freezer

Factory Details

21,000 cu.ft.
3 White fish fillet lines
1 Red fish fillet line
3 APV Clark H.P. Freezer able to freeze 20 tons per day
Shetland type 28 gutter

Baader Equipment

1 type 412 header	2 type 188 filleters
2 type 421 headers	3 type 47 skinners
1 type 99 filleter	1 type 150 fillet/header for red fish

Engine Details

English Electric Co. Ruston Paxman Eng. Div.	Type 16 RK3CH Diesel 2600 BHP 13½ knots

Launched	Skipper Maiden Voyage	Crew No.
1st March 1971	John Dobson	33

Named by

Mrs Mary Purdy, stepmother of Mr. J.F. Purdy, Chairman Ranger Fishing Co.

Company's Marine Superintendent, Les Abbey, had an office in Tromso and could help with the ship's progress.

In 1973 due to P. & O. Shipping Company coming out of

fishing, the new Ranger Calliope with her sisters became part of the B.U.T. fleet at Hull and was renamed Kelt.

In August 1981 Kelt was sold out of fishing by B.U.T. to Norwegian owners and after a massive refit she barely resembled her original form, having become a Marine Diving Support Depot Vessel.

Now Bergen Survivor, Norwegian Diving Depot Ship
X Sub Surveyor 1984
X Sub Surveyor One 1983
X Kelt 1982

RANGER CALLISTO

Ranger Callisto was delivered in February 1972 and sailed

Name	Reg. No.	Off. No.	Tons	Length/Breadth	Call Sign
Ranger Callisto	SN17	338108	1106	216.9	GPAG
Kurd	H 242		411	40.2	

Builder	Type
Brooke Marine Ltd. Lowestoft 1972	Factory freezer

Factory Details

21,000 cu.ft.
3 White fish fillet lines
1 Red fish fillet line
3 APV Clark H.P. Freezer able to freeze 20 tons per day
Shetland type 28 gutter

Baader Equipment

1 type 412 header	2 type 188 filleters
2 type 421 headers	3 type 47 skinners
1 type 99 filleter	1 type 150 fillet/header for red fish

Engine Details

English Electric Co. Ruston Paxman Eng. Div.	Type 16 RK3CH Diesel 2600 BHP 13½ knots

Launched	Skipper Maiden Voyage	Crew No.
24th June 1971	Bill Bowman	33

Named by

Dame Irene Ward, M.P. for Tynemouth

from North Shields for her maiden voyage at the beginning of March. She was commanded by Skipper Bill Bowman and fished the Norwegian coast and White Sea grounds for a 3 month trip, landing 300 tonnes of fillets.

In 1973 Ranger Callisto stood by the Ranger Aurora, which had broken down and was in danger of drifting into the Fortes Oil Field. After a few hours the Aurora got safely underway again.

The Ranger Callisto was the third in a class of four trawlers, which were nicknamed the "Floating Hiltons" due mainly to the striking livery of the trawlers and the crew receiving soap and bed linen and being able to watch films. They also had a sheltered working trawl deck. This combined to give some misguided people the impression that life on the stern trawlers was easy compared to sidewinders. They seem to forget crews could be away for up to 100 days in all weathers on factory freezers.

One novel aspect of Ranger Fishing Co's operation was that during slack fishing if she had not caught her quota of fish after 100 days, the ship was called into Tromso and her crew flown home for leave, and a new crew flown out. The ship would then take on stores and fuel and finish her trip.

The leaving crew would receive their cash on the share of what they had caught on arriving home.

In August 1973 Ranger Callisto became the 1st of the former Ranger fleet to arrive at their new home port of Hull. She received the B.U.T. name Kurd.

The Kurd was on hand to help two British freezer trawlers who had fallen victim of fire.

On the 1st May 1974 Kurd with Skipper John Dobson rescued the crew of the Grimsby freezer Victory which was on fire off the Norwegian coast. In April 1975 Kurd towed home the fire gutted Orsino, from the Norwegian port of Honningsvaag. This tow took ten days during south west gales. Kurd's best fishing year was 1978 when she was the 14th Top British Freezer.

In 1981 Kurd was sold to Norwegian owners for conversion into a diving support vessel.

Now Southern Surveyor, Norwegian Diving Depot ship.
X Kurderen 1982
X Kurd 1981

RANGER CASTOR

Ranger Castor was the 4th ship of Ranger's "C" class and the last ship built for the Ranger Company. She was bought by B.U.T. on the 15th October 1973.

The Disappearance of the Gaul

The Gaul sailed from Hull on the 22nd January 1974 commanded by Skipper Peter Nellist. She stopped off at Bridlington to pick up an extra sparehand, making the crew

Name	Reg. No.	Off. No.	Tons	Length/Breadth	Call Sign
Ranger Castor	SN 18	338111	1106	216.9	GPAH
Gaul	H 243		411	40.2	

Builder	Type
Brooke Marine Ltd.	Factory
Lowestoft 1972	Freezer

Factory Details

21,000 cu.ft.
3 White fish fillet lines
1 Red fish fillet line
3 APV Clarke H.P. Freezers able to freeze 20 tons per day in 7 & 14lb blocks, graded for quality and size
Shetland type 28 gutter

Baader Equipment

1 type 412 headers	2 type 46 skinners
2 type 421 headers	3 type 47 skinners
1 type 99 filleters	1 type 150 fillet/header
2 type 188 filleters	(for reds)

Engine Details

English Electric
Ruston Paxman Diesel
Type 16RK3CH
2600 BHP 13½ knots

Launched	Skipper Maiden Voyage	Crew No.
6th December 1971	George Saul	33

Named by

Mrs J. Bailey, wife of a Director of P. & O.

up to 36 men. Gaul then proceeded to the Norwegian fishing grounds.

On the 26th January she put into Lodingen, Norway, where her mate who had become ill was put ashore. Then on 28th January she put into Tromso to pick up a replacement mate. The next nine days were spent fishing off the North Cape in the company of other trawlers. During the night of the 7th-8th February weather conditions very rapidly deteriorated, with gale force winds. Despite the excellent sea-keeping qualities of the modern stern trawlers, they had to suspend fishing operations and dodge into the wind to maintain their positions in the fishing area.

On the morning of the 8th February, the Gaul and Swanella's mates who were friends spoke to each other over V.H.F. radio whilst they were in a position 3 to 4 miles apart. Gaul then steamed past Swanella to dodge in a different position. This was the last time she was seen by a British trawler.

Photo by courtesy of Walter Fussey & Son.

At 09.30 Gaul reported on her office schedule to her owners that she was laid dodging as were 11 other ships. Then at 10.30 she reported to the support ship Othello on the Skipper schedule and at just after 11.00 Gaul sent two private messages through Wick radio. From then what happened to Gaul has become a maritime mystery, which has been much speculated on but never satisfactorily solved.

The majority of Hull trawlermen believe the Gaul was either overwhelmed by one or more massive freak waves, or that water had built up in her factory deck, due to hoses being left running or a watertight door being left open. This could cause a combination of excessive free surface water on her trawl deck and on the main factory deck. In heavy weather this could have caused her to capsize.

The Men Missing with the Gaul:

R. Atkinson; C. Briggs; R. Bowles; S.J. Broom; J. Chisholm; R. Chisholm; P. Clark; S. Collier; J. Doone; B. Dudding; J. Gardner; E. Grundy; T. Hackett; J. Haywood; W. Jones; T. Magee; J. McLellan; C. Naulls; P. Nellist (Skipper); R. Nilsson; J. North; J. O'Brien; J.R. O'Brien; N. Petersen; J. Riley; T. Sheppard; C. Smith; M. Spurgeon; K. Straker; T. Tracey; J. Wales; D. Wheater; J. Woodhouse; H. Wilson; A. Warner; H. Wood:

ROSS GROUP

In 1895 Thomas Ross founded what was to become a very successful fish merchanting company at Grimsby. Two sons joined the business and, due to Thomas Ross falling ill, J. Carl Ross directed the Company. His efforts were so successful that his father handed the Company to him in 1928.

The Company then ordered the first all-electric diesel powered trawler, the "British Columbia", and formed Grimsby Motor Trawlers Ltd. This was managed by Sir Alec Black, who had built up his own fine fleet. On his death his fleet was bought by Ross's.

In 1945 a major step was taken with the acquisition of 66% shares of Trawlers Grimsby Ltd., and, in 1948 all interests of Thomas Ross were transferred to that company. Also in 1948 the Hull company Charleson-Smith was acquired. In 1958 Ross Group Ltd. was formed to cover all the Company's activities.

In the mid 1960s, Ross Group had a fleet of 65 trawlers at Hull and Grimsby, consisting of new ships built at Cochranes of Selby which was part of Ross Group and the fleets of several companies acquired by Ross Group. Mr. J. Carl Ross was Chairman of Ross Group from 1928-1968. His son, John M.R. Ross, became Managing Director of Ross Trawlers.

In 1969 Ross Group, under Chairman A.S. Alexander, merged with Associated Fisheries to form British United Trawlers.

NAMES: Various themes with the Ross prefix.
FUNNEL: Black top, grey with green flag containing a white star
HULL: Black, also grey.

INVINCIBLE

(Ross) Invincible was the fourth of the 4 sister trawlers ordered by Ross Group and given warship names. But due to being built after Ross Group's amalgamation into B.U.T. the Ross prefix was dropped. Invincible was Hull's 23rd Freezer trawler and sailed from Hull on her maiden voyage on the 30th October 1970, commanded by Skipper Roy Waller, in a trip to the White Sea Grounds. She returned after a 7 week trip with just under 400 tonnes of frozen blocks.

In 1972 the British Trawler Federation produced a league table of Top Freezer Trawlers which later became the Dolphin Bowl Competition. Invincible was the top British trawler with 2692.1 tonnes, 40,910 points. Her sister ship, Ross Vanguard, was second with 2107.8 tonnes, 34,178 points.

During October 1973 Invincible and her sisters, Ross Illustrious and Ross Implacable, were transferred to Grimsby. This meant that all 6 Ross Group Freezers were now sailing from Grimsby. The reason for this move was that Grimsby's market was unable to meet the demand for pre-frozen fish and catches were having to be transported from Hull.

In 1978 B.U.T. sent Grimsby's last 6 freezers to Hull ending the port's 15 years of freezer stern trawler opera-

Name	Reg. No.	Off. No.	Tons	Length/ Breadth	Call Sign
Invincible	H 96	339814	1085	234.0	GOMV
			487	39.6	

Builder	Type
Cochrane & Sons Selby 1970	Wholefish Freezer

Factory Details

28,800 cu.ft.
2 fish holds 1fd. 1 aft of engine room
12 x 12 Station Jackstone Froster V.P. freezers
Capable of freezing 30 tons per day

Engine Details

English Electric
Ruston Hornsby
Type 9 ATCM
2160 BHP 14½ knots

Launched	Skipper Maiden Voyage	Crew No.
7th April 1970	Roy Waller	26

Named by

Mrs G. Sacher, wife of a Director of Marks & Spencer

tions. Invincible was transferred back to Hull on the 2nd July 1978.

In 1982 Invincible, along with 11 other freezers, was sold out of the British Fishing Industry. Nine of these became stand-by vessels. Invincible was sold to Seaboard Offshore Ltd., Inverness and was converted in 1983.

Photo by courtesy of T. J. M. Wood.

Now Seaboard Invincible (Standby safety and oil pollution recovery vessel).
X Invincible 1982

ROSS ILLUSTRIOUS

Ross Illustrious was the second of a class of four sister trawlers built by Cochranes for the Ross Group. The shipyard was one of many companies within Ross Group and in the 1960's built many fine trawlers for the parent company.

Roy Waller was chosen as her Skipper having won the Silver Cod in 1963 and 1964, and being runner up in 1965 in the Ross Leonis. Ross Illustrious was Hull's 11th freezer trawler.

The Ross Illustrious sailed from Hull on her maiden voyage on the 29th September 1966 and went to the New-

Name	Reg. No.	Off. No.	Tons	Length/Breadth	Call Sign
Ross Illustrious	H 419	308560	1076	234.0	GTRA
			354	39.6	

Builder	Type
Cochrane & Sons Ltd.	Wholefish
Selby 1966	Freezer

Factory Details

2 fishroom 1 forward 1 aft 35,000 cu.ft.
2 banks of 6 x 12 Station Jackstone Froster V.P. Freezers capable of freezing 30 tons per day

Engine Details

Ruston Hornsby Ltd.
Type 9 ATCM
2150 BHP 14 knots

Launched	Skipper Maiden Voyage	Crew No.
6th April 1966	Roy Waller	26

Named by

Mrs G. Black, wife of the Chairman of Mac Fisheries

foundland grounds. Due to running-in troubles she had to make calls into St. Johns for repairs. This cut down her fishing time and lengthened her voyage, arriving back in Hull after 58 days with just over 300 tonnes of mainly codstuffs.

In January 1972 Ross Illustrious went to the aid of the Grimsby sidewinder, Hull City, which had developed engine trouble whilst homeward bound off the North East coast of Scotland. In very rough seas a tow was attached and Ross Illustrious towed her into Buckie. Hull City went on to land 2,000 kits at Grimsby.

In October 1973 Ross Illustrious and her 2 Hull based sisters were transferred to Grimsby to boost Grimsby's frozen fish market needs. She sailed from Grimsby until the 30th June 1978 when she was transferred back to Hull where dock dues were lower.

In 1979 it was proposed to sell Ross Illustrious to Nigeria which had already bought Ross Vanguard, but due to problems being encountered by Ross Vanguard with freezing in high sea temperatures the sale fell through.

Ross Illustrious was acquired by Seaboard Offshore of Inverness in 1982 for conversion to a standby safety vessel for pollution control and firefighting capabilities for offshore installations.

Now Seaboard Illustrious, standby vessel.
X Ross Illustrious 1982

ROSS IMPLACABLE

Name	Reg. No.	Off. No.	Tons	Length/ Breadth	Call Sign
Ross Implacable	H 6	334090	1042	234.0	GYUH
			452	39.6	

Builder	Type
Cochrane & Son Ltd.	Wholefish Freezer

Factory Details

2 fishrooms 1 forward 1 aft 35,000 cu.ft.
2 banks of 6 x 12 Station Jackstone Froster V.P. Freezers
capable of freezing 30 tons per day.

Engine Details

Ruston Hornsby
Type 9 ATCM
2160 BHP 14 knots

Launched	Skipper Maiden Voyage	Crew No.
16th March 1968	George Whurr	25

Named by

Mrs J.D. Sainsbury, wife of the Vice Chairman of
Sainsbury's

At the time of her launch, Ross Implacable was the heaviest
ship to enter the Ouse at Selby. It was the first time Cochranes had installed all the auxilliary and refrigeration plant,
also fire prevention equipment, in a ship before its launch.
She cost £500,000 to build and the Government gave a 40%
grant towards the cost. Ross Implacable ran her trials off
the Humber on the 24th September 1966.

On leaving her berth to begin her fourth voyage, as Mr.
Charles Hudson watched the proceedings from his office
window through the fog, he was astonished to see her
suddenly charge ahead dragging her tugs with her. She hit a
trawler a glancing blow but the tugs managed to steer her
through the gap between the moored trawlers and pulled
her up just short of the end of the dock. After adjustments
she proceeded on her trip.

In 1969 Ross Implacable was B.U.T.'s top Hull trawler
catching an impressive 3,781 tonnes in only 284 days at sea.

On the 4th February 1972 Ross Implacable was towed
into Bergen after engine failure, by the Grimsby sidewinder
Lord Beatty. On the 10th December 1974 she was towed
home from Spitzbergen after engine trouble.

Ross Implacable was transferred to Grimsby from Hull

Photo by courtesy of Steve Pulfrey.

in October 1973 in a B.U.T. fleet reorganisation, and then back to Hull from Grimsby on the 14th September 1978.

In 1982 Ross Implacable was sold to Iranian owners for fishing in the Indian Ocean.

Now Hamoor 1
X Ross Implacable 1982

ROSS INTREPID

Cape Kennedy was to be the last of the long line of "Capes" built for Hudson Bros, which became part of the Ross Group in 1960. She was Ross Group's first Hull freezer stern trawler, sister to Ross Valiant of Grimsby.

She sailed on her maiden voyage from Hull on the 12th March 1965. Skipper Neilson took Cape Kennedy to the Labrador and Newfoundland fishing grounds. She landed back in Hull after a 46 day trip, with a capacity catch of 400 tonnes of cod. On the trip she had steamed an estimated 5,000 miles.

In March 1966 in accordance with Ross Group's decision to name their freezer trawlers after warships, Cape Kennedy was renamed Ross Intrepid.

On the 6th February 1967 Ross Intrepid whilst steaming to Newfoundland hit a wave which flooded her forepeak and chain locker. Because the bilges were clogged with potatoes, carrots and onions from the f'ward stores, the crew had to bail out the water by hand. After completing fishing, on her return home it was noticed that her bow was moving. On her return to Hull she had to go into William Wright dry dock for repairs.

Name	Reg. No.	Off. No.	Tons	Length/ Breadth	Call Sign
Ross Intrepid	H 353	305780	1156	226.6	MHTD
Cape Kennedy			531	36.7	

Builder	Type
Cochrane & Sons Ltd.	Wholefish
Selby 1965	Freezer

Factory Details

22,000 cu.ft. fish hold
10 Station Jackstone Froster V.P. Freezers
2 rows, 5 port, 5 starboard capable of freezing 30 tons per day in 100lb blocks

Engine Details

Mirrlees National Ltd.
Type JLSSM 8
2650 BHP 13 knots

Launched	Skipper Maiden Voyage	Crew No.
12th June 1964	Ken Neilson	26

Named by

Mrs Hudson, wife of Mr. Tom Hudson, Managing Director of Hudson Bros.

In February 1968 Ross Intrepid was damaged by ice below the waterline during a trip to Newfoundland, but she was able to cope and on her return to Hull landed 390 tonnes before going for repairs.

In October 1968 in a fleet reorganisation Ross Intrepid was transferred from Hull to Grimsby but she retained her Hull registration number.

In 1969 she became part of the B.U.T. fleet, until 1975 when along with her sister Ross Valiant she was laid up as uneconomic, because of their small fishrooms. Buyers were sought and later in the year Ross Intrepid was sold to Norwegian owners.

Now Malene Ostervold, Bergen, Norway. Seismographic survey ship, converted from fishing in 1978.

X Ross Intrepid 1975
X Ross Kennedy 1966
X Cape Kennedy 1966

ROSS VALIANT

Name	Reg. No.	Off. No.	Tons	Length/ Breadth	Call Sign
Ross Valiant	GY 729	304793	1156	226.6	MHKV
			528	36.7	

Builder	Type
Cochranes & Sons Ltd. Selby 1964	Wholefish Freezer

Factory Details

22,000 cu.ft. fish hold
10 Jackstone Froster V.P. freezers
2 rows, 5 port 5 starboard able to freeze 30 tons of fish per day in 100lb blocks

Engine Details

Davy Paxman & Co. Ltd.
Diesel Electric
Type 8YLCZ
1650 BHP 13 knots

Launched	Skipper Maiden Voyage	Crew No.
30th January 1964	Jack (Jock) Kerr	26

Named by

Mrs L.M. Harpergow, wife of a Ross Group Director

Ross Valiant was Grimsby's first freezer stern trawler and at the time of her launch she was the biggest of the 1500 ships built by Cochranes in 75 years of shipbuilding. She sailed on her maiden voyage from Grimsby on the 24th

June 1964, commanded by Skipper Jock Kerr. He took Ross Valiant to fish at the Labrador fishing grounds. After a trip of 35 days she returned to Grimsby with a capacity catch of 400 tonnes, equal to 6400 kits.

After the loss of the three Hull trawlers and grounding of Notts County at Iceland during January and February 1968, on the 7th February the Government ordered British trawlers to leave the fishing grounds between Isafjord and Langanes. On the 9th February Ross Valiant was chosen to be temporary control ship to which Skippers at Iceland had to report every 12 hours. But next day it was decided instead to use one of the M.O.D. weather ships which was on station in the Atlantic and allow Ross Valiant to continue in her fishing role.

On the 23rd May 1969 Ross Valiant went to the aid of a

small Norwegian fishing boat which laid stricken and damaged off Scotland in the North Sea. The big Ross Valiant provided a lee shelter, while a fleet of twelve small Norwegians put pumps on board and attached a tow line to make for port.

On the 10th November 1970 Ross Valiant went to the aid of the Hull trawler C.S. Forester which was disabled after a fire in the engine room. From a position 200 miles off Tromso, Ross Valiant towed the stricken vessel into Harstad Norway.

In 1969 Ross Valiant, along with the rest of the Ross Group fleet, became part of British United Trawlers fleet. During May 1975 Ross Valiant along with her sister ship Ross Intrepid was laid up by B.U.T. as uneconomic due to her small fishroom. In September 1975 Ross Valiant was sold to Faroese Skipper, Johan A. Plogv, for shrimp fishing at Greenland.

Now Avoq, registered at Godthab, Greenland.
X V.W. Hammershaimb 1981
X Ross Valiant 1975

ROSS VANGUARD

Ross Vanguard was the first of a class of four trawlers built at Selby. She was delivered in May 1966. For her maiden voyage she fished the Newfoundland grounds commanded by Skipper Jack (Jock) Kerr, who had pioneered Ross Group's freezer work in Ross Valiant. She returned home to Grimsby after six weeks to land 450 tonnes of blocks.

Name	Reg. No.	Off. No.	Tons	Length/Breadth	Call Sign
Ross Vanguard	GY 1372	307561	1488	234.0	GSLE
			643	39.6	

Builder	Type
Cochrane & Sons Selby 1966	Wholefish Freezer

Factory Details

28,800 cu.ft.
2 fish hold 1 fd 1 aft of engine room
12 x 12 Station Jackstone Froster V.P. Freezers capable of freezing 30 tons per day

Engine Details

Ruston Hornsby Ltd.
Type 9 ATCM
2150 BHP 14½ knots

Launched	Skipper Maiden Voyage	Crew No.
14th October 1965	Jack Noble Kerr	23

Named by

Mrs E.D. Young, wife of a Director of Ross Group

For her size Ross Vanguard was a successful ship. She was runner-up Champion Trawler in 1972, and in 1975 landed 8 full trips and was halfway through another by the year-end. In one of the fastest trips by a freezer, just 28 days, she landed 530 tonnes of mainly cod from the Norwegian and White Sea grounds.

In 1974 after the research trawler Cirolana had found variable amounts of Blue Whiting between Ireland and Faroe, B.U.T. sent Ross Vanguard for a 10 day trial dip in the area as a test, before continuing on her normal trip to the Norwegian coast and White Sea grounds. The small amount of blue whiting caught was used for tests.

As can be expected of ships that spend nearly all their lives at sea, Ross Vanguard encountered some problems. In December 1972 her steering gear broke down off the North Cape of Norway and she was towed home by a Norwegian salvage tug. The 1300 mile tow was undertaken in bad weather conditions and it took over two weeks to bring her home. At one stage it took 12 days to cover what could have been steamed in 2½ days. Then in August 1978 Ross Van-

Photo by courtesy of Steve Pulfrey

122

guard, with Skipper Peter Costello, went to the aid of the stricken trawler Roman, taking off 10 survivors while the Goth towed Roman into Honningsvaag.

In happier days in January 1973 Ross Vanguard's regular Skipper Jock Kerr was awarded the M.B.E. for his service to the industry. After doing three weeks of a trip to the Norwegian coast he was relieved by Skipper Wally Boden at Vardo and flown home to go to London for the investiture on the 5th March 1973.

On the 25th June 1978 Ross Vanguard was transferred to Hull, but kept her Grimsby registration. On the 28th August 1979 she was bought by Nigerian owners who planned to buy the other three ships in her class, but due to problems with overheating in tropical waters only the Ross Vanguard was acquired.

Now Aramoko, fishing from Nigeria
X Ross Vanguard 1982

INDEX OF FISHING REGISTRATION NUMBERS
ISSUED TO STERN TRAWLERS

HULL

H

3	Boston York	242	Kurd
6	Ross Implacable	243	Gaul
31	St. Jasper	249	Junella (2)
40	Southella	269	Princess Anne
86	C.S. Forester	301	Northella (1)
96	Invincible	308	St. Finbarr
135	Farnella	330	Lord Nelson
137	Seafridge Osprey	347	Junella (1)
138	Seafridge Skua	353	Cape Kennedy (Ross Intrepid)
144	Dane	362	Arctic Freebooter
150	Pict	367	Kirkella
164	St. Benedict	384	Marbella
175	Seafridge Petrel	385	Sir Fred Parkes
177	Cordella	389	Othello
180	Hammond Innes	397	Lady Parkes
188	Arctic Buccaneer	398	Cassio
193	Norse	410	Orsino
195	Arctic Galliard	412	Coriolanus
206	Northella (2)	419	Ross Illustrious
233	Turcoman	421	Swanella
236	Esquimaux	436	St. Jason
237	Afghan	440	Arctic Privateer
238	Arab	441	Arctic Raider
240	Kelt	442	St. Jerome

GRIMSBY

GY

252	Goth	1364	Conqueror
253	Roman	1372	Ross Vanguard
729	Ross Valiant	1377	Defiance
733	Victory	1399	Boston Lincoln

NORTH SHIELDS

SN

14	Ranger Boreas	30	Ranger Briseis
15	Ranger Cadmus	147	Ranger Ajax
16	Ranger Calliope	148	Ranger Apollo
17	Ranger Callisto	149	Ranger Aurora
18	Ranger Castor		

THE HULL STERN TRAWLER FLEET
THE BUILDING OF THE FLEET 1961-1975

Year	New Buildings	Joining Hull Fleet	From	Leaving Hull Fleet	To
1961	Lord Nelson				
1962	Junella				
1964	Northella St. Finbarr				
1965	Arctic Freebooter Cape Kennedy Kirkella				
1966	Cassio Lady Parkes Marbella Orsino Othello Ross Illustrious Sir Fred Parkes			St. Finbarr	Lost
1967	Coriolanus St. Jason Swanella				
1968	Arctic Privateer Arctic Raider Boston York Ross Implacable St. Jerome			Ross Intrepid X Cape Kennedy	Grimsby

Year	New Buildings	Joining Hull Fleet	From	Leaving Hull Fleet	To
1969	C.S. Forester St. Jason Southella				
1970	Invincible				
1971		Boston Lincoln	Grimsby		
1972	Farnella Hammond Innes Seafridge Osprey Seafridge Skua				
1973	Cordella Dane Northella (2) Pict Princess Anne St. Benedict Seafridge Petrel	Ranger Apollo-Turcoman Ranger Aurora-Esquimaux Ranger Boreas-Afghan Ranger Cadmus-Arab Ranger Calliope-Kelt Ranger Callisto-Kurd Ranger Castor-Gaul	North Shields " " " " " "	Boston York Junella (1) Northella (1) Invincible Ross Illustrious Ross Implacable	Canada South Africa South Africa Grimsby Grimsby Grimsby
1974	Norse			Gaul	Lost
1975	Arctic Buccaneer Arctic Galliard Junella (2)			Seafridge Osprey	Norway

THE GRIMSBY FREEZER STERN TRAWLER FLEET 1964-1978

Year	New Buildings	Transferred to Grimsby	Transferred from Grimsby	Lost
1964	Ross Valiant			
1965	Conqueror Victory			
1966	Defiance Ross Vanguard			
1968	Boston Lincoln	Ross Intrepid		
1971			Boston Lincoln to Hull	
1973		Invincible Ross Illustrious Ross Implacable		
1974	Goth Roman			Victory
1975			Ross Intrepid to Norway Fishing Ross Valiant to Greenland fishing	
1977			Conqueror to Hull Defiance to Hull	
1978			Goth to Hull Invincible to Hull Roman to Hull Ross Illustrious to Hull Ross Implacable to Iran Fishing Ross Vanguard to Nigeria Fishing	

THE DECLINE 1976-1985

Year	Vessels out of Hull Fleet	New Role	Transferred to Hull	Lost
1976	Seafridge Skua Arctic Privateer	To Norway Fishing To Min. Ag. & Fish Research		
1977	Esquimaux Hammond Innes Lady Parkes Othello Seafridge Osprey Turcoman	Standby Work To Canada Fishery Research To France Survey Work To Australia Fishing To Norway Fishing Standby Work	Conqueror Defiance	
1978	Cassio Orsino	To Australia Fishing To Australia Fishing	Goth Roman Ross Illustrious Ross Implacable Ross Vanguard Invincible	Conqueror
1979	Afghan Marbella	To Scrap (Marr) Survey Work		
1980	C.S. Forester Coriolanus Lord Nelson	To Iceland Fishing To Greece Fishing To Scrap		
1981	Princess Anne Southella Swanella	To Canada Survey Work (Marr) Survey Work To Norway Standby Work		

Year	Vessels out of Hull Fleet	New Role	Transferred to Hull	Lost
1982	Arctic Buccaneer Arctic Galliard Cordella Kelt Kurd Farnella Northella (2) Ross Illustrious Ross Implacable Ross Vanguard Invincible Sir Fred Parkes	To New Zealand Fishing To New Zealand Fishing To New Zealand Fishing To Norway Diving Support To Norway Diving Support (Marr) Survey Work (Marr) Survey Work Standby Work To Iran Fishing To Nigeria Fishing Standby Work Standby Work		
1983	Arab Junella (2)	To Norway Diving Support To Greenland Fishing		
1984	Arctic Raider Dane Goth Kirkella Norse St. Benedict	To Iran Fishing To Panama Survey Work To Norway Fishing Standby Work To Norway Fishing To New Zealand Fishing		
1985	Arctic Freebooter Boston Lincoln Defiance Roman St. Jasper St. Jerome St. Jason	(Boyd) Standby Work To Panama Standby Work Standby Work To Greenland Fishing Standby Work Standby Work To Holland fishing		
1986	Pict	To Guernsey Fishing		

During a tour of the Hull and Grimsby fish docks in July 1978 H.R.H. the Prince Charles visited the "Junella". Pictured with Prince Charles are Mr. Andrew L. Marr and Skipper Charles Drever MBE. Photo by courtesy of Walter Fussey & Son.

TOP FREEZERS

Year Ending

1967	Marbella	3784 tons
1968	Lady Parkes	3790 tons
1969	Lady Parkes	4169 tons
1970	*No details*	
1971	Southella	2574 tons
1972	Invincible	2692 tons
1973	Dane	2911 tons
1974	Arctic Freebooter	3400 tons
1975	Norse	3093 tons
1976	Arctic Galliard	4363 tons
1977	Arctic Galliard	4139 tons
1978	Arctic Buccaneer	6272 tons
1979	Arctic Buccaneer	No details
1980	Arctic Galliard	No details

DOLPHIN BOWL CHARTS

1973

		Tons	Points
1	Dane (B.U.T.)	2,911.3	46,738
2	Farnella (Marr)	2,684.6	42,636
3	Arctic Freebooter (Boyd)	2,476.4	39,089
4	St. Jason (Hamlings)	2,315.7	36,837
5	Defiance (B.U.T. Gy)	2,392.3	35,936
6	Coriolanus (B.U.T.)	2,345.9	35,384
7	Kirkella (Marr)	2,144.1	34,545
8	Swanella (Marr)	2,126.7	33,902
9	Marbella (Marr)	2,083.6	33,564
10	Conqueror (B.U.T. Gy)	2,156.4	32,111

1974

		Tons	Points
1	Arctic Freebooter (Boyd)	3,400.6	51,177
2	Lady Parkes (Boston)	2,787.8	42,684
3	Defiance (B.U.T. Gy)	2,878.4	41,326
4	Farnella (Marr)	2,954.4	41,218
5	Southella (Marr)	2,658.9	40,225
6	Cordella (Marr)	2,704.7	38,982
7	Pict (B.U.T.)	2,672.1	38,553
8	St. Jasper (Hamlings)	2,598.6	37,826
9	Swanella (Marr)	2,443.1	37,399
10	Dane (B.U.T.)	2,581.7	36,811

1975

		Tons	Points
1	Norse (B.U.T.)	3,093.9	48,777
2	Southella (Marr)	2,723.2	46,110
3	St. Jerome (Hamling)	2,761.4	43,445
4	Cordella (Marr)	2,608.4	41,960
5	Princess Anne (Boston)	2,630.7	41,072
6	St. Benedict (Hamling)	2,596.0	40,501
7	Arctic Freebooter (Boyd)	2,765.0	39,718
8	Dane (B.U.T.)	2,488.9	39,415
9	Seafridge Petrel (Newington)	2,466.4	39,301
10	Swanella (Marr)	2,367.0	38,505

1976

		Tons	Points
1	Arctic Galliard (Boyd)	4,363.7	52,483
2	Norse (B.U.T.) estimated	2,983.3	46,711
3	Junella (Marr)	2,931.3	46,459
4	Farnella (Marr)	2,835.0	43,069
5	Dane (B.U.T.)	2,723.8	42,650
6	St. Jerome (Hamling)	2,712.5	39,793
7	Lady Parkes (Boston)	2,491.1	39,059
8	St. Jasper (Hamling)	2,601.8	38,922
9	Goth (B.U.T., Gy)	2,375.7	36,923
10	Arctic Buccaneer (Boyd) estimated	2,310.4	35,451

1977

		Tons	Points
1	Arctic Galliard (Boyd)	4,139.1	35,472
2	Princess Anne (Boston)	4,375.0	34,438
3	Orsino (B.U.T.)	3,916.4	32,629
4	Dane (B.U.T.)	2,133.6	32,033
5	Arctic Buccaneer (Boyd)	2,699.0	31,187
6	Southella (Marr)	2,786.8	30,218
7	Northella (Marr)	2,733.0	28,664
8	Arctic Freebooter (Boyd)	2,046.8	28,600
9	St. Jason (Hamling)	2,684.6	28,569
10	Farnella (Marr)	2,288.1	28,528

1978

		Tons	Points
1	Arctic Buccaneer (Boyd)	6,272.1	37,696
2	Arctic Galliard (Boyd)	5,344.5	39,614
3	Northella (Marr)	4,579.6	28,808
4	St. Benedict (Hamling)	5,529.7	28,524
5	Southella (Marr)	4,421.7	28,295
6	Arctic Freebooter (Boyd)	2,383.1	26,636
7	Pict (B.U.T.)	1,570.5	24,869
8	Princess Anne (Boston)	4,049.1	24,234
9	Defiance (B.U.T.)	4,534.1	23,397
10	Dane (B.U.T.)	1,631.8	22,477

PERSONALITIES

(Above) Five "Skippers". Left to right: Dick Taylor, Terry Thresh, Tom Nielsen, Jack Lilley and Roy Waller.

Skipper Jack N. Kerr MBE, who pioneered freezer stern trawling out of Grimsby in 1964.

The presentation of the 1976 Dolphin Bowl. Left to right: Captain B.T. Wortley, Tom Boyd and Roy Waller.

Joint Dolphin Bowl presentation in 1979. Left to right: Thomas W. Boyd, Stan Barwick, Terry Thresh, Commander Ayre and Andrew L. Marr. Photo by courtesy of Walter Fussey & Son.

The Hull Challenge Shield presentation in 1975 (for year 1974). Pictured left to right: Mr. Lionel Cox, Mr. Richard Cox (Hull F.U.O.A.), Mr. Bill Suddaby (B.T.F.), Mr. Alan Marr, Mr. Andrew Marr (Marr's), Commander Ayre, Mr. Mike Burton, Mr. Les Abbey (Newington's), Skipper Bill Brettell (winner), Mr. Derek Oswald (B.U.T.), Mr. D. Chapman (Marr's), Skipper Terry Thresh, Mr. George Hartley (B.U.T.), Skipper Tom Nielsen and Sir Basil Parkes.

INDEX

Note: Each index entry refers to a ship's position in the main table only.

Afghan H237	107	Invincible H96	115	Ranger Callisto SN17	111
Arab H238	109	Junella 1 H347	82	Ranger Castor SN18	113
Arctic Buccaneer H188	46	Junella 2 H249	84	Roman GY253	59
Arctic Freebooter H362	47	Kelt H240	110	Ross Illustrious H419	116
Arctic Galliard H195	48	Kirkella H367	85	Ross Implacable H6	118
Arctic Privateer H441	50	Kurd H242	111	Ross Intrepid H353	119
Arctic Raider H440	51	Lady Parkes H397	39	Ross Valiant GY729	120
Boston Lincoln GY1399	36	Lord Nelson H330	33	Ross Vanguard GY1372	121
Boston York H3	37	Marbella H384	86	St. Benedict H164	61
C.S. Forester H86	94	Norse H193	56	St. Finbarr H308	62
Cape Kennedy H353	119	Northella 1 H301	88	St. Jason H436	64
Cassio H398	71	Northella 2 H206	89	St. Jasper H31	66
Conqueror GY1364	30	Orsino H410	73	St. Jerome H442	69
Cordella H177	78	Othello H389	75	Seafridge Osprey H137	99
Coriolanus H412	72	Pict H150	58	Seafridge Petrel H175	101
Dane H144	53	Princess Anne H269	40	Seafridge Skua H138	101
Defiance GY1377	32	Ranger Ajax SN147	103	Sir Fred Parkes H385	41
Esquimaux H236	105	Ranger Apollo SN148	104	Southella H40	91
Farnella H135	81	Ranger Aurora SN149	105	Swanella H421	92
Gaul H243	113	Ranger Boreas SN14	107	Turcoman H233	104
Goth H252	55	Ranger Briseis SN30	108	Victory GY733	34
Hammond Innes H180	97	Ranger Cadmus SN15	109		
Hausa	108	Ranger Calliope SN16	110		